Famous Hispanic Americans

ACKNOWLEDGMENTS

We would like to thank our editor for her continual assistance during this project. We are also grateful to Dr. Carlos E. Cortés, for contributing the informative and insightful Foreword.

We greatly appreciate the interviews (oral or written) and assistance granted by the following participants in this volume: Felipe Alou, Jaime Escalante, Gloria Estefan, Gigi Fernandez, Carolina Herrera, Lourdes Lopez, Ellen Ochoa, and Ileana Ros-Lehtinen.

We also thank the following: Monique Giroux and Richard Griffin, Media Directors for the Montreal Expos, Ruth Ruiz, Los Angeles Dodgers Press Department, and Dr. Joseph Quarles for providing major/minor league information; Jaime W. Escalante, Jaime A. Escalante's son, who assisted with information and provided photographs, Carl Smith of the Foundation for Advancements in Science and Education; Becky Fajardo, sister of Gloria Estefan, and staff assistants at Estefan Enterprises, Inc.; Carol Baird of the Fred Scharf Marketing Group and Tom Yamaguchi of Yonex Corp., Racquet Sports Division; Andy Garcia, and Henry Acuna and Rose Fahey; Roberto C. Goizueta, and The Cola-Cola Company; Deborah Hughes, Director of Public Relations, Carolina Herrera, Ltd.; Liz Healy and the staff assistants in the New York City Ballet Press Department; Dr. Antonia Novello, and Dr. M. Ann Drum and Shellie Abramson; Rosanne Ochoa, mother of Dr. Ellen Ochoa, who loaned family photographs, Tammy West at NASA, and the NASA Johnson Space Center for providing biographical data and technical information; Secretary of Transportation Federico Peña, and Joyce Craley, Julie Case, and Constance Gray in the Department of Transportation, and Stan Oliner and Margaret Walsh of the Colorado Historical Society; Superintendent Matt Rodriguez, and Police Officer Salvador Martinez, Aide to the Superintendent, Chicago Police Department; Paul Rodriguez, and Levine/Schneider Public Relations; and Richard Chabran, librarian, and the staff of the Chicano Studies Research Library at UCLA.

We especially appreciate the support of members of our families, Jack Morey, Bruce Dunn, and Julie Dunn. We also extend special thanks to Allen Michel, our legal advisor.

PREFACE

From baseball to ballet, the U.S. Congress to outer space, Hispanic Americans contribute to every area of our society. Each of the fourteen outstanding Hispanic Americans presented in this book is an individual whose story reflects his or her background, choices, and determination.

Those profiled represent a wide variety of fields, including government, science, business, law enforcement, education, sports, the arts, and entertainment. Their achievements span from winning an Olympic Gold Medal to serving as a Cabinet Secretary.

The heritages and experiences of these prominent Hispanic Americans are varied. Some were born in the United States, others came to this country as children or elected to relocate as adults. Felipe Alou is from the Dominican Republic, Jaime Escalante came from Bolivia, and Carolina Herrera was born in Venezuela. After Fidel Castro gained power, a number of Cubans left for the United States, including Gloria Estefan, Andy Garcia, Roberto Goizueta, Lourdes Lopez, and Ileana Ros-Lehtinen. Gigi Fernandez and Antonia Novello were both born in Puerto Rico. Ellen Ochoa, Federico Peña and Matt Rodriguez were all born in the United States and have Mexican ancestry, as does Paul Rodriguez, who immigrated from Mexico.

While most of these fourteen are U.S. citizens, citizenship was not a criterion for inclusion. In every case, these individuals have lived and worked in the United States and contributed significantly to our culture. Their influence has also stretched around the world.

Choosing notables for a volume such as this is always difficult, as there were many distinguished Hispanic Americans to consider. In making selections, advice and suggestions were solicited from around the country. Some Mexican Americans who were recommended for inclusion already appear in an earlier book, *Famous Mexican Americans* (Cobblehill Books, 1989) also by Morey and Dunn.

The authors were privileged to interview or correspond with many of the people in this work, and were fortunate to receive photographs from both personal and professional collections. In all cases,

the subjects themselves or their designated aides reviewed and approved the material in their own chapters.

For each individual, accomplishments are explained, while motivations are traced, often from childhood. A reader may gain insights from personal anecdotes, while a young researcher is provided with a wealth of information. How were goals reached? Were there any setbacks or sacrifices? Each story is unique.

FOREWORD

Hispanics or Latinos? The terminology debate goes on . . . and on . . . and on. But call them what you will, they—Americans of Latin American and Iberian ancestry—have become increasingly important in the story of the United States. And they will certainly play an even more critical role in our nation's future.

Part of the story rests on demographics. For example, in 1989 the U.S. Census Bureau projected that the Latino/Hispanic population of the United States would increase nationally by 187 percent between 1990 and 2030, compared with a 25 percent population increase for white Americans, a 68 percent increase for African Americans, and a 79 percent increase for Asian Americans, Pacific Island Americans, and American Indians. Of course, these are merely educated guesstimates. Unpredictable events, such as changes in immigration laws or the passage of the North American Free Trade Agreement, might serve to modify those projections. However, while the *rate* of population change might be altered, the demographic *direction* of the United States is clear. Day by day, our nation is becoming more multiethnic, particularly more Latino.

However, neither the past, the present, nor the future is one of just numbers. It is also one of people. This book addresses Hispanic people, their achievements, and their contributions.

The book deals with Latinos . . . or Hispanics, if you prefer. In truth, those two terms serve merely as linguistic conveniences to embrace Americans of different Latin American and sometimes Iberian (Spanish and Portuguese) ancestries. U.S. Latinos come from diverse origins. They may be Mexican Americans, Puerto Ricans, Cuban Americans, Guatemalan Americans, or Chilean Americans. Some come from multiple Latino ancestries—for example, a Mexican-American mother and a Cuban-American father. Or they may be only partially of Hispanic background, as some one-third of U.S. Latinos now marry persons of other backgrounds.

Hispanics have become part of the United States in different ways. Some entered the United States through annexation: the 1845 U.S. annexation of the Republic of Texas; the 1848 U.S. annexation of one-third of Mexico, including most of present-day California, New Mexico, and Arizona, through the Treaty of Guadalupe Hidalgo at the close of the U.S.-Mexican War; the 1854 Gadsden Purchase of what is today southern Arizona and New Mexico; or the 1898 Treaty of Paris following the Cuban-Spanish-American War, which changed the status of Puerto Rico from a part of the Spanish empire to a part of the United States.

Even more Latinos have become part of the United States through immigration. Most have come to escape poverty, seeking the dream of economic advancement. Others have come with excellent Latin American educations, looking for the opportunity to maximize the use of their knowledge, skills, and creativity. Some have come as political refugees, fleeing revolution, turbulence, or various forms of oppression. And they have come from different nations, bringing with them their unique Latin American cultures.

Finally, millions of Latinos have been born in the United States. Some even trace their U.S. ancestry back to the middle of the nineteenth century. Latinos, then, are a widely diverse people.

But if Hispanics are so diverse, does it make any sense to talk about them as a group? Yes. Although Latinos reflect various heritages and experiences, Hispanics of different national-origin backgrounds still share many cultural tendencies.

Except for Brazilians (and Portuguese, if you include Iberians), most Hispanics are linked by a common language of heritage, Spanish, although many U.S. Latinos do not speak Spanish. They tend to be Catholic, although Protestantism and other religions are growing rapidly in Latin America and among Latinos in the United States. Hispanics tend to have powerful attachments to *la familia* (the extended family). They tend to have a strong sense of *comunidad* (community). They often share traditional Hispanic values and practices, such as *compadrazgo* (inherited or adopted kinship), *personalismo* (a strong sense of personalism), *dignidad* (dignity), and *orgullo* (pride).

Latinos also share something else. Whether annexed, immigrants, or U.S.-born, they have contributed greatly to our nation. They have harvested food and have popularized it in thousands of Latino restaurants. They have labored tirelessly in mines and factories. They have built railroads and created businesses. They have worked in offices, served in hospitals, and taught children of all backgrounds. They have excelled in sports, entertainment, and the arts. The United States has become a better nation because of the contributions of Latinos.

Contributions should never be confused with fame. Most people, including most Hispanics, who contribute do not become rich or famous. Important family and community contributions have been made by thousands of Latinos, whose names unfortunately will never appear in newspapers, television newscasts, or history books. Most of us know such people and should honor them for their deeds.

But anonymity has not been the fate of all Latinos. Some Hispanics, because of their intelligence, skills, creativity, leadership, and efforts have made special achievements that have earned public recognition. This book reveals the accomplishments of some of those Latinos.

The story of the United States remains incomplete if it fails to include the stories of Latinos as well as people of other ethnic backgrounds. The lives of Hispanic women and Hispanic men make up an essential part of the American experience. By relating the stories of selected Hispanic women and men who have made noteworthy contributions and achievements, this book helps to fulfill the American Dream of inclusiveness, the dream of a nation that honors its diversity as a way of furthering its unity.

CARLOS E. CORTÉS
Professor of History
University of California, Riverside

Dr. Carlos E. Cortés was born in Oakland, California. He received his Ph.D. in history from the University of New Mexico and is Professor of History at the University of California at Riverside. He has chaired Latin American Studies, the Chicano Studies Program, and the History Department, all at UC Riverside. Dr. Cortés has written and edited numerous books and articles. His special areas of interest include Latin American history, ethnic history, and multicultural education.

CONTENTS

Felipe Alou

Throughout the history of baseball there have been several brother combinations playing in the same league. The first trio of note had the last name of DiMaggio—Joe, Dominic, and Vince. However, a claim to further fame was established by Felipe, Matty, and Jesus Alou in September, 1963, when they became the first trio of brothers to play on the same team, covering the left, right, and center-field positions for the San Francisco Giants.

Felipe Alou recalls: "It was a great thrill to be on the same team with my two younger brothers. Three brothers playing together is something that was never accomplished before. Even thirty years after it happened, it still hasn't been accomplished again."

In the following year, Felipe Alou left his brothers when he was traded to the Milwaukee Braves. During his seventeen-year career he was a player on seven different major league teams. By 1974, at the end of his playing years, he had been selected to play in three All-Star Games, had a career batting average of .286, and became the thirty-first player in baseball history with over 2,000 hits and 200 home runs.

The end of his impressive playing career did not signal retirement from baseball for Felipe Alou. In 1976, he began a new career as a spring training instructor for the Montreal Expos in Daytona Beach, Florida. In the following years, he became a team manager in the minor leagues, mainly the Florida State League and the Dominican Winter League.

In early 1992, Felipe Alou joined the Montreal major league staff as the Expos' bench coach and, a few months later, was promoted to team manager. When Felipe Alou became manager of the Expos, this event was noted in baseball history books. He is the first baseball manager in the major leagues born in the Dominican Republic and the fourth Hispanic American. The first three Hispanic managers, Mike Gonzalez, Preston Gomez, and Cookie Rojas, were all born in Cuba. Felipe Alou is also recognized as the fifth person in the major leagues to be in a manager-player, father-son position. His son, Moises Alou, is an outfielder for the Expos.

Felipe Alou, manager of the Montreal Expos

Felipe Rojas Alou was born to Jose Rojas and Virginia Alou on May 12, 1935, in the outskirts of Santo Domingo, the capital city of the Dominican Republic. In Latin-American countries, children often carry two last names. First comes the last name of their father and then the last name of their mother. However, when Felipe joined the Giants organization he, and later his younger brothers, became known by the last name of Alou only. Felipe was the eldest of six children. Most of his childhood days were spent attending elementary school, helping in his father's blacksmith and carpentry shop, and going fishing with his father to catch fish for the family's meals.

Felipe's first school went up to grade six and was the only school in the area. His class had to stay in the sixth grade for one additional year until the secondary school was built. He remembers his favorite subjects were geography and history. He especially liked learning about the history of the Dominican Republic, the native West Indians, and the exploration of the Americas. During this time, baseball was a Saturday or Sunday informal game with three or four kids playing against three or four others. Sometimes girls played with them. "Every time I went to play baseball my father didn't like it very much. He thought I was not very interested in helping him at the shop. In the 1940s, when I was nine, ten, and twelve years old, my parents considered baseball as good exercise but not as a profession. It, especially, was not a profession that parents would encourage their oldest son to choose."

When Felipe was thirteen, he went on a special school trip that he will never forget: "My teachers took our class to see the Dodgers play a spring training game. In 1948 and 1949, the Dodgers and the Montreal Royals, a Triple A team, came to the Dominican Republic for spring training. I saw Roy Campanella, Pee Wee Reese, Jackie Robinson, Duke Snider, Gil Hodges—it was really great! I believe that seeing this game really had a lot to do with me being a baseball player today."

It was not until high school that Felipe Alou played a baseball game with nine players against another nine. At this time, an uncle gave Felipe his first baseball glove of his own. There was only one high school and games would be organized with teams within the school playing against each other. When the second high school was built in Santiago on the other side of the island, the two high school teams competed.

In addition to baseball, Felipe Alou became involved in track and field. He ran relays and learned to throw the javelin. In 1954, he was selected to attend the Central American Games in Mexico City. Felipe Alou remembers that his team did not do very well. He only had three months' experience throwing the javelin and he had to compete against the best javelin throwers in all of Central America. Felipe felt fortunate to go to Mexico and to be able to mix with athletes from other countries. In the following year, Felipe was again chosen to represent his country, this time in the Pan American Games. Knowing he did not have a good chance in the track and field events, Felipe only played baseball. "We won the Gold Medal. We beat the

U.S. team in the final game—10 to 4. I'll never forget that score."

After the Pan American Games, several baseball organizations became interested in signing a player's contract with Felipe Alou. However, a special rule existed under Rafael Trujillo, then head of the Dominican government, that applied to aspiring athletes. Before signing a professional contract, athletes were obligated to represent the Dominican Republic in at least three international competitions. After the Pan American Games, Felipe Alou had to wait one more year to participate in his third competition in Venezuela.

In 1956, Felipe Alou signed his first professional baseball contract with one of the San Francisco Giants' farm teams. Being the oldest son, Felipe sent the $200 bonus that was given to him upon signing to his parents. "Being the oldest hurt and helped. I always had to work harder than the other kids. Even after I signed my first contract, I sent most of my paycheck home to help buy food for my family. I am very proud of myself and also my two younger brothers who played baseball in the United States. But they did not have to send any money back home to pay the bills because I had already taken care of that."

Being the first of the Alou brothers to play baseball in the United States, Felipe was also the first to tackle the challenge of learning English. He had learned some English throughout his schooling. However, he found that the English he had studied was different from the English he actually encountered. Felipe remembers riding in a Florida cab from the airport with an older player from the Dominican Republic who spoke English: "I was listening to the conversation but I did not understand anything. I heard the cab driver say over and over, 'Yeah, yeah.' I asked the player who accompanied me, 'What is yeah? I never heard this word in school.' He said that it means, 'Yes.' Why did I go to school to study English if it is different? I'm not a person who watches much TV or listens to the radio, but I learned English by practicing. By summer, I was able to survive in English. I could order food, buy clothes, catch a bus, argue with the umpire . . ."

In 1958, Felipe Alou was brought up from the minor leagues to play on the San Francisco Giants team. He batted and threw right-handed and played outfield with other Latino teammates such as Ossie Virgil, Ruben Gomez, Orlando Cepeda, and Ramon Monzant, as well as with Giants great, Willie Mays. In his first full season, he established himself as an excellent major league hitter with a batting average of .275 and 33 RBIs (runs batted in). Between 1958 and 1974, Felipe Alou played for the Giants, the Milwaukee Braves, the Atlanta Braves, the Oakland A's, the New York Yankees, the Montreal Expos, and Milwaukee Brewers.

In addition to playing in the same outfield with his two brothers, another highlight from Felipe Alou's career was playing in all seven games of the

1962 World Series. Although the Giants lost the World Championship to the New York Yankees, they had already won the National League Pennant in an exciting division play-off series: "In the ninth inning of the last game we were losing 2–4. We scored four runs, beating the Dodgers 6–4 and winning the National League Championship. When we looked around the stands you couldn't hear one sound. All of the 52,000 baseball fans in Dodger Stadium were dead silent . . . That was a great feeling because of the intense rivalry between the Dodgers and the Giants."

After retiring as players, all three Alou brothers have continued to work in the baseball organization. Matty Alou is with the San Francisco Giants' minor leagues and Jesus Alou is working with one of the Florida Marlins' minor league teams. In 1976, Felipe Alou was invited to become an instructor for the Expos at their spring training in Daytona Beach, Florida. He began his managerial career the following year. Over the next twelve years he achieved a record of 844 wins and 751 losses, managing five different minor league teams. During this time, his teams finished in first place three times and won two league championships. In 1990, Felipe Alou was honored as Manager of the Year with an impressive 92–40 record in the Florida State League.

When Felipe Alou became major league manager of the Montreal Expos in 1992, he rekindled the team's winning spirit. The Expos became con-

Felipe Alou urging his team on to victory

tenders for the divisional title instead of allowing the preseason predictions of finishing in last place to come true. Felipe attributes his progress to being a major league player himself, his successful coaching experiences in the minor leagues, and knowing each of the player's strengths. One of the Expo players who presents a special challenge is his son, Moises Alou. "Coaching my son is very interesting. It is not an easy position for him or for me. I have to be fair with everybody. I have to be a little stricter with the way I handle Moises because I don't want anyone to think that I am favoring my son. But I don't want to overtax him either because I need to be honest with him. The one thing that makes my job and his job a little easier is that he is a very good player."

Felipe Alou has worked hard to achieve his present position as a major league manager. He feels that he must set a good example for other minorities who will follow him in his role as a professional manager. He advises students not to give up when meeting certain obstacles. "When I first came to Florida, people would ask me where I was from. I would tell them the Dominican Republic and they didn't know where it was. I felt like a person without a country. Some people would make jokes about my accent or my color. As a minority, I know it is especially important to do

Felipe Alou with Expo player and son, Moises Alou

things well. It has taken me a lot of sorrow, a lot of joy, discouragement, encouragement, a mixture of ups and downs to get to this manager's position. I have to be at my best physically and mentally and to always stay prepared for any opportunity which may arise."

According to Felipe Alou, the best way young people can prepare is by developing good character traits. Doing a good job, even when no one is watching, being obedient, and completing any work with pride are some ways to build strong character. "As a manager in the minor and major leagues, I have received high school and college players. They each bring their character with them. It has already been developed when they are young children. By the time they join the team it is too late to build character. I only have time to teach people to play baseball." Felipe Alou has found that the players who come to him with strong character are generally able to increase their skills more rapidly and to excel in their careers.

During the baseball season, Felipe Alou can be found at his home in Montreal with his wife, Lucie, and their young daughter and son. However, he spends the most time in airplanes and in hotels while traveling for away games with the Expos' team. The rest of the year is divided between his homes in Boynton Beach, Florida, and the Dominican Republic. Baseball and his nine children from four marriages keep him busy. He lost one of his ten children, Felipe II, in a tragic swimming pool accident in 1976. Even with a full schedule, he tries to find time to contact his many fishermen friends. Although he enjoys every kind of fishing, deep-sea fishing is his favorite. "My number one love is fishing in the ocean because I come from the islands. I feel freer out in the deep sea—far from the noises of other people. When I am fishing I can really relax and forget all the troubles of life."

Felipe Alou's list of honors continues to grow. In his first year as rookie manager of the Montreal Expos, he was voted second for National League Manager of the Year by the Baseball Writers Association of America. In 1994, before the baseball strike brought the season to a close, he led his team to achieve the best record of wins and losses in the major leagues. This winning record also earned him the title of National League Manager of the Year, having 27 of the 28 first-place votes. With two full careers in one lifetime, Felipe Alou has made many celebrated contributions to baseball fans and baseball history.

Jaime Escalante

In this scene the hero is surrounded and outnumbered. He must be very careful. One wrong move could result in a great loss. He turns quickly to rearm himself—with a piece of chalk and a calculus book.

Our hero is a high school math teacher, who is determined to motivate his very unmotivated students to learn. His students later demonstrate their excellence by passing the almost impossible AP (Advanced Placement) exam in calculus. Less than 2 percent of students in the United States attempt this difficult mathematics test. This is the first time that so many students from this inner city high school are able to pass the exam. The Educational Testing Service (ETS) officials become suspicious of the scores and have the students take a second, harder exam. Passing the second test, the students, Jaime Escalante, and the parents prove to the nation that they are able to "take a stand and deliver."

This 1988 movie, *Stand and Deliver*, is based on the true story of teacher Jaime Escalante and his math students at Garfield High School in East Los Angeles. After months of overcoming obstacles such as lack of parent involvement, poor nutrition, expectations of failure, and gang influences, eighteen students passed the Advanced Placement Calculus test in 1982. This marked only the beginning. In the following years, the number of students enrolled in Jaime Escalante's math classes and able to pass the final AP exam steadily increased. By 1991, over 300 Garfield High School students had completed Escalante's program and about 160 had taken the test. Edward James Olmos' striking portrayal of Jaime Escalante in *Stand and Deliver* resulted in an Oscar nomination for Best Actor. Actors Lou Diamond Phillips, Rosana De Soto, and Andy Garcia were also featured in the movie.

Born in La Paz, Bolivia, on December 31, 1930, Jaime Alfonso Escalante Gutierrez was the second of five children born to Zenobio and Sara Escalante. His parents were schoolteachers who worked for a time in Achacachi, a small Aymara Indian village. At the age of nine, his family returned to La Paz where young Jaime spent the rest of his childhood and continued his schooling. After graduating from San Calixto, one of Bolivia's top high

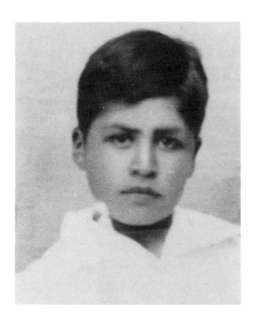

Jaime Escalante at about age nine at his First Communion.

schools, Jaime Escalante entered Normal Superior, a teacher's college. According to Escalante, he felt math and physics were his strongest subjects. Although his first choice in careers had been engineering, his parents could not afford the tuition for that school.

Normal Superior College helped Jaime Escalante to become more focused and disciplined in his studies. "I did not find school to be fun, from an academic point of view. I received a good background in physics and math. My professors recognized my ability to solve problems, usually using my own and different methods."

Jaime Escalante was fortunate to complete his

teacher training under an excellent instructor. He carefully observed his instructor's way of interacting with students and the methods of teaching used, and his own style of teaching began to take shape. He learned to keep trying new approaches until student success is increased and to discontinue the programs that do not work. Having his stu-

Left to right: Friends V. Carbajal and R. Maldonado with Jaime Escalante on August 6, Bolivian Independence Day, at San Calixto High School.

dents actively participate in their learning instead of watching the teacher stand at the chalkboard all day made a difference. He obtained a strong understanding of the subject matter to be taught, so he could show students how learning is important in their own lives.

In addition to his college studies, Jaime Escalante held part-time teaching jobs at three different high schools, as well as tutoring students who needed extra help. After graduating from Normal Superior College in 1954, he began teaching math and physics at the high school level. Also in this same year, he married a fellow Normal Superior graduate, Fabiola Tapia. Their first son, Jaime, Jr., was born in La Paz on September 27, 1955. Over the next nine years, Jaime Escalante developed his first group of science teams. These tenth through twelfth graders from San Calixto High School were able to win many competitions against other challenging schools in the city.

The U.S. State Department sponsored a special, one-year program for Latin-American teachers. With the aid of a scholarship, Escalante attended this program at the University of Puerto Rico in Rio Piedras from 1960 to 1961. During this period, he was able to extend his travel to include a trip covering Washington, D.C., Pennsylvania, New York, and some cities in Canada. After returning to Bolivia, Fabiola suggested immigrating to the United States where some of her relatives had relocated. She felt there would be greater career opportunities for her husband and, in the future, for her son. She was also concerned about the unstable economic and political situation in Bolivia at that time with many strikes and several revolutionary attempts to overthrow the government. In 1964, Jaime Escalante moved to Pasadena, California, knowing just a very few words of English. Fabiola and Jaime, Jr., joined him five months later in that same year.

It was not an easy beginning for the Escalantes.

Jaime Escalante, at about the time he made his first visit to the U.S.

Although a college graduate and experienced teacher, Jaime Escalante would need to earn an American college degree to regain the professional level he had achieved in Bolivia. He worked as a busboy, a cook, and then as an electronics factory technician, attending school at night to complete courses toward another college degree. In whatever job he undertook, he was continually thinking of new ideas. While working as an electronics technician for the Burroughs Corporation, he designed several cost-saving devices to improve quality control. During this time, the Escalantes' second son, Fernando, was born on July 14, 1969.

Almost ten years after Jaime Escalante relocated to Pasadena and at the age of forty-three, he was able to earn a bachelor's degree in math and physics as well as a teaching credential from California State University, Los Angeles. Rather than continuing in his job with Burroughs, he decided to take a cut in salary and return to teaching. "I always had in mind to eventually go back to teaching."

In 1974, Jaime Escalante walked through the doors of Garfield High School, eager to begin his first teaching assignment in the United States. The school is located in a predominantly Hispanic area of Los Angeles that has contributed to high rates of crime, gang violence, drug abuse, and school dropouts. The majority of students in Mr. Escalante's math courses made the opening weeks of school especially challenging. Many students were disinterested, discourteous, and often late or absent from class. Not willing to give in or to give up, Jaime Escalante decided on a plan. He would put his beliefs into practice and all his energy into redirecting these students onto a more productive path.

According to Jaime Escalante, the following requirements and responsibilities are crucial to student success:

Accountability—The teacher, along with parental and administrative support, is responsible for the success or failure of the students.

Hard Work—This is necessary by both the teacher and the students to make the future.

Demand—I do not allow my students to be losers and, given the chance, they will be winners.

Parental Involvement—Parents must help but sometimes it is more difficult when both parents work, one parent is missing from the home, or they do not believe in the value of education for their children.

Respect and Values—I teach the kids respect for themselves and values that will uphold their family, school, community, race, culture, and country.

Nutrition—If more attention was paid to what kids eat and to ensuring that they were properly nourished before and during the school day, we would see real dividends in student performance.

Prevention of Drug Use—Drug use is a barrier to classroom performance. I tell my students to go toward their goals aggressively, refusing to let anyone steer them into drugs.

Love and Caring—The power of love and concern in changing young lives should not be overlooked.

In the movie *Stand and Deliver*, as well as in real life, Jaime Escalante actively promotes *"ganas,"* meaning desire or will to succeed. *"Ganas* suggests a powerful urge to get ahead, a willingness to sacrifice and to work hard. *Ganas* conquers all. *'Ganas* Is All I Need' is the motto I give my students. I tell them that once they have *ganas*, learning is easy. *Ganas* is a desire that must emerge from within." In his classroom, Mr. Escalante selects a certain spot that students see most often to post his motto—next to the clock on the wall.

When most people are winding down in their careers, Jaime Escalante, now over sixty, is doing just the opposite. In 1991, he made the decision to leave Garfield High School and to start over at Hiram Johnson High School in Sacramento. Unwilling to compromise his beliefs to improve his relationship with several staff members, combined with a need to see if his beliefs could also take root in a different school setting, he chose a new home. Garfield has a majority Hispanic student population of about 3,400 students with approximately 25 percent of the families on welfare. Hiram Johnson has about 1,000 less students, an ethnic mix of about one-third non-Hispanic white, one-third Asian, one-third black and Hispanic, with approximately 35 percent of the school's families on welfare. When Jaime Escalante asked the Sacramento school superintendent to transfer to the new district, he did not demand an increase in his salary or benefits. He did request including at least two

Jaime Escalante, educator

basic math or algebra classes in his teaching schedule, so that he could begin the groundwork for calculus. The year before he arrived at Hiram Johnson only six students took the AP Calculus test. In four years he plans to increase this number to one hundred.

In addition to giving time to help math students before school, during lunch, after school, and on Saturdays, Jaime Escalante is involved with programs outside of his school. In 1983, he began a summer work-study program in partnership with East Los Angeles College (ELAC). Funded in part by the ARCO Foundation and the National Science Foundation, the eight-week program allowed students to earn money by working half day and to learn math, physics, biology, chemistry, or English by attending classes for the other half of the day. Some students worked for ELAC and ARCO, while others held part-time jobs at hospitals, universities in the area, and the Jet Propulsion Laboratory (JPL) in Pasadena. After moving to Sacramento, Jaime Escalante designed a summer study program for Hiram Johnson students which includes classes as well as field trips to different industries to show how math is used in the workplace. Over the years, hundreds of students have profited from these unique opportunities.

Another area that consumes Jaime Escalante's time is video and television programming to promote careers in math and science. Millions of students across the nation have viewed or have access to these special programs on the Public Broadcasting Service (PBS) channels. "Futures" and "Futures²" are a series of programs designed to show students how math is used in their daily lives and the variety of available careers that involve math, such as renewable energy, graphic design, computer software programming, meteorology, astronomy, fashion, and environmental engineering. First released in 1990, these programs have received over twenty broadcasting and educational awards, including the respected Peabody Award.

The U.S. Department of Energy, NASA, ARCO, and the Foundation for Advancements in Science and Education (FASE) are among those who have continued interest in Escalante projects. They have provided generous funding and/or assistance with program production. One program entitled "Living and Working in Space: The Countdown Has Begun" was televised in March, 1992, on PBS and presented the near-future possibilities of living and working in space. Escalante's "Multimedia Math Project" is one of his most recent accomplishments. Professionals in math-related jobs are interviewed by Jaime Escalante and two other expert math teachers. To be available in video, it is intended as a resource for teachers, who can use it for enrichment of a particular idea or lesson.

From 1988 to 1992, Jaime Escalante served as a consultant on the President's Educational Policy Advisory Committee. As a consultant to the National Science Foundation Advisory Board, he traveled to Washington, D.C., several times a year to discuss ways to increase interest in science at the high school and college levels. He continues to be actively involved with the Fund for Excellence in Education, which produces science resources and educational videos for schools across the country. For his many contributions and accomplishments, Jaime Escalante has been awarded seven honorary doctoral degrees by colleges across the country.

As time allows, Jaime Escalante enjoys working on home projects, especially those involving carpentry. He also likes to read different types of math books. When he watches sports events, highlights later appear as examples in his lessons or become math problems for his students to solve.

With each group of students, Jaime Escalante shares an important message: "Remember, you have to decide what you want to be in life. No one person can tell you what you want to be. Go forward toward your goals. People are always watching you and learning from you. You are the best. You can be whatever you want to be. Do you want to be a winner or a loser? Keep in mind that you do not enter into success; *you make* the success. Go forward with *ganas*. Believe in your dreams."

Gloria Estefan

On August 24, 1992, Hurricane Andrew thundered through Miami, Florida, cutting a wide path of destruction with powerful 135 mph winds and extensive flooding. Many people were left homeless without food or clothing. In the wake of this disaster, two people were very lucky to suffer only damage to the landscaping at their Star Island home and Miami business establishments. In return for their good fortune, Gloria and Emilio Estefan opened a relief center at their south Miami offices; collected donated food, water, and diapers; and coordinated a volunteer group to distribute these items to those in need. As the lead singer of the award-winning group, Miami Sound Machine, Gloria Estefan was able to give even more: "I was very happy that my husband, Emilio, and I were able to successfully organize a concert for and with our community which generated over two million dollars for the hurricane victims."

Gloria Estefan was born to Jose Manuel and Gloria Fajardo on September 1, 1958, in Havana, Cuba. Named after her mother, a schoolteacher, Gloria was nicknamed "Glorita" meaning "little Gloria." Her father worked for the President of Cuba, Fulgencio Batista y Zaldivar, as a member of the army team that protected and provided security for the President's family. In 1959, Batista was forced out of power and Fidel Castro became the Prime Minister of Cuba. Fearing for their safety under the Castro regime, the Fajardos immigrated to the United States. They first settled in Texas for a short time where the Fajardos' second daughter, Becky, was born when Gloria was six years old.

The Fajardo family's next home was in Miami. Many Cuban exiles, refugees, and immigrants relocated to a particular area of this city which later became known as "Little Havana." Here, Gloria began school. She spoke mostly Spanish at home and learned English from her friends and teachers. Graduating from Our Lady of Lourdes Academy, an all-girls school, Gloria went on to receive her bachelor's degree in psychology from the University of Miami. Gloria's mother also learned English, so she could resume her teaching career. Her father joined the U.S. Army where he achieved the rank of Captain. After returning from two years of duty in Vietnam, he developed multiple sclerosis, a disease that attacks the brain and spinal cord, causing tremors and loss of coordination.

Gloria's childhood and teenage years were often difficult as she recalls: "I was extremely shy as a child. My life was filled with studying for school, nursing my father, and baby-sitting my little sister until my mom came home from work each day. In the afternoons, after school and helping dad, I would close my bedroom door and play the guitar and sing. This was my escape from everyday life and singing gave me pleasure."

Gloria's schooling was very important to her. She learned to speak English and French fluently, in addition to her native Spanish. When Gloria was old enough to work, her first job was as a translator at the Miami International Airport, speaking both Spanish and English. She also enjoyed reading and began to write poetry. Her love for music overlapped her interest in writing. "I used to make up new lyrics to songs which were popular. These songs are called parodies. I would sing the parodies for my friends and we would all laugh together."

While attending the University of Miami, she met Emilio Estefan. Like the Fajardos, the Estefans also fled Cuba when the new government took over their privately owned business. Emilio eventually relocated to Miami where he continued to be hardworking and enterprising. After starting several small businesses of his own, he decided to work for a large company, Bacardi Imports, which markets rum from the Caribbean islands. His first job was in the mail room, and because of his dedication and interest, Emilio was quickly promoted to higher and higher positions. Soon he worked his way up and became a company executive as director of the Bacardi Latin markets. During his corporate rise, Emilio also pursued his interest in music. As a child, he taught himself to play the accordion and later became a percussionist. He organized a band called the "Miami Latin Boys," which practiced in his aunt's one-car garage in-between performances at private parties. While providing the entertainment at one of these private parties, he heard Gloria Fajardo sing and decided to add a female lead vocalist to his group.

Gloria aspired to become a psychologist; however, her life plans took a different turn. "I did not choose my career, my career chose me. I was singing on weekends with a small Latin band at weddings and parties, and soon we began to write our own music, and through something that started as a sidekick, I soon found it would be my lifelong profession. I never dreamed that I would be a recording artist when I was young. This goes to show that sometimes you don't have to look so hard for a good thing, it may be right there underneath your nose. All you have to do is see it."

In a few short years after Gloria joined the Miami Latin Boys, their popularity grew and Gloria worked hard to overcome the shyness that made her feel so uncomfortable in the spotlight. She also followed a rigorous exercise and diet program

Emilio and Gloria Estefan in a publicity photo for the 1993 American Music Awards program.

which she continues today. Extra pounds were shed and an athletic body developed for energetic performances and music videos requiring physical stamina. The group's versatility in providing lively Cuban dance music called "salsa" as well as Top 40 hits propelled them into fame and a new name—"Miami Sound Machine."

By the end of 1978, Gloria had graduated from college and Miami Sound Machine had produced their first album featuring English and Spanish songs, including original songs written by different members of the group and sung in Spanish. During this year, Gloria and Emilio were married. Worried about risking their successful working relationship, their love developed slowly after a comfortable and special friendship had been established. Looking back, they recall that in order to save money, they did not have a music band or a wedding reception. Two years later, major and exciting changes again occurred. Gloria and Emilio's son, Nayib, was born, Emilio quit his executive job with Bacardi Imports to promote the group, and a recording contract was signed with CBS Records, a powerful company with the ability to distribute records worldwide.

During the 1980s, CBS records promoted Miami Sound Machine throughout Latin America, including Mexico, Argentina, Brazil, Peru, Venezuela, Honduras, Costa Rica, El Salvador, and Panama. Their albums reached the number one position in several of these countries. The hit song that helped expand Miami Sound Machine's tours beyond Miami and throughout American and European countries is entitled "Conga." The conga is a traditional Cuban line dance done to music featuring conga drums and a strong Latin and African beat. Whenever the group performed this upbeat song at one of their concerts, audiences could not resist forming conga dance lines that sometimes numbered in the hundreds and thousands.

Although "Conga" was a big success, it did not climb any higher on the Pop Charts than number ten. The group's first number to reach the top of the Charts was a sentimental ballad called "Anything for You" on the *Let It Loose* album. Gloria remembers in amazement that she wrote this song while getting a quick bite to eat. As soon as she arrived in the recording studio, the producers added the music and in less than twenty-four hours the song was completed. The record company did not feel that it was strong enough to include on the album, but Gloria as the songwriter and Emilio as part of the production team, believed in the potential of this song and convinced Epic Records otherwise. "Anything for You" remained on the hit charts around the world for almost a year. After recording this album, Emilio retired from performing as the group's percussionist and began to develop his music production company more fully. Emilio's clientele list grew with popular artists such as Julio Iglesias, Clarence Clemons from the Springsteen E Street Band, and Jon Secada.

Gloria Estefan performing in concert

Live concerts and traveling, as well as recording sessions, consume much of a performer's time. It was during one 1990 tour which included a snowy stretch of highway between eastern Pennsylvania and a concert stop in Syracuse, New York, that the Estefans became involved in a terrible bus accident. Fortunately, Emilio and their son, Nayib, escaped without serious injury; Gloria was not as lucky. When the semi-truck struck their bus from behind, Gloria was thrown to the floor and her back was broken. After surgery, extensive physical therapy, and an endurance of pain, Gloria Estefan made a remarkable recovery. Before 1992 arrived, she had already released the album *Into the Light* which eventually produced five Top Ten hits and became her fourth album to sell more than one million copies. During 1991 she also started the highly successful "Into the Light" tour with concerts in many parts of the world—Europe, Southeast Asia, Australia, South America, Central America, and Mexico—entertaining over two million people.

With celebrity status goes the need to balance family and public obligations. Gloria focuses her attention on being a good mother and wife as well as continuing to write quality, meaningful songs to sing and to record more albums for people to enjoy. Her concentrated efforts as a songwriter have earned Gloria Estefan multiple Grammy Award nominations, the American Music Award, and BMI Songwriter of the Year. "I am especially proud that I have been recognized as a songwriter with the BMI award I received in 1989. You see, it is one thing to be able to sing and entertain, and another completely different one to be recognized as a songwriter. Songwriters are sometimes the 'unsung heroes' of music making and it takes a lot of insight and community awareness to be able to write songs that appeal to the masses."

Recognized as an international superstar who has sold over twenty million records, has had seventeen Top Ten hits, completed four world tours, and earned over $45 million during 1991–92, Gloria Estefan pauses to reflect on responsibilities and sacrifices: "Sacrifices come with all choices in life. My sacrifices lie in the fact that I travel often, and am not able to spend as much time with my family as I would like. Of course, when you are in the public eye, as I am, you sacrifice the fact that your life is not as personal as most others. It is my responsibility to myself to be a good example for people and to use my public image to try to make this a better world for everyone."

Gloria Estefan has volunteered her time in the community and given concerts in a variety of settings. In addition to assisting victims of Hurricane Andrew, she has participated in a youth, antidrug campaign. Billboards with Gloria Estefan cautioning children to "Say No to Drugs!" have reinforced this important message. Her efforts in substance abuse education earned special recognition and appreciation from former President George Bush. Reaching people of all ages and backgrounds has been a goal for Gloria Estefan and the Miami Sound Machine. One way this has been accomplished is through performances at different sporting events, such as the Olympics in Seoul, Korea; the World Series; the Pan American Games; and the Super Bowl. Another way has been through giving special performances for or receiving invitations from heads of state and royalty during the Miami Sound Machine's world concert tours. Former President George Bush, Prince Charles and Princess Diana, former Philippines President Corazon Aquino, and Princess Elena of Spain have enjoyed the spirited Latin beat and romantic ballads of Gloria Estefan and the Miami Sound Machine.

Today, the Estefans maintain their residence and business in Miami. Before moving to their home on Star Island, they lived on Miami Sound Machine Boulevard, which was renamed in their honor by the Miami City Council. Emilio Estefan has cultivated his talents as a music producer while

Gloria Estefan

transforming his recording studio into an accomplished multimillion-dollar business. The Estefans' interests have also expanded into the Miami restaurant business. Their family grew with the birth of daughter Emily Marie in 1994.

Throughout her career, Gloria Estefan has traveled to many countries and has learned about many different cultures. These experiences have enabled her to develop a sensitivity toward the feelings that people share around the world which are reflected in her songwriting. The lyrics of her songs have universal appeal and the music rhythms highlight her Hispanic heritage. In her message to young readers, Gloria Estefan has chosen to share the chorus from "Nayib's Song (I Am Here for You)" written for her son:

I am here for you, and you are here for me
It's an ongoing process.
I will take care of you and you will take care of me
If we're gonna make some progress.

Words and music by Gloria Estefan,
© 1991 Foreign Imported Productions and Publishing, Inc.

"We all need to work together to make this world a safe, happy, and clean place. By taking care of each other through concern for your family and neighbor, we can join together and accomplish great things. In the end we will be preserving our planet and society for future generations to come."

Gigi Fernandez

Winning the Gold Medal at the Olympics was the most memorable event of my career. What is so special about this is that everybody can relate— everybody knows the Olympics and everybody knows what a Gold Medal is. After coming home, people would come up to me in restaurants and pat me on the back. They would say, 'You made us so proud! You did it for us!' It was a feeling that I had done something, not for myself, but for our country and all the people and it was very special. Every time I hear 'The Star-Spangled Banner,' I still get emotional and a big smile comes to my face as I remember that moment . . ."

Gigi Fernandez has been recognized as the world's top women's player in doubles tennis. In 1992, she and Mary Joe Fernandez (no relation) won the Olympic Gold Medal for doubles tennis in Barcelona, Spain. Between 1988 and 1993, Gigi Fernandez won over thirty-five doubles tennis titles, including the superior achievement of nine Grand Slam tournament championships. In accomplishing this remarkable record, Gigi Fernandez has played with doubles teammates such as Robin White, Martina Navratilova, Jana Novotna, and Natalia Zvereva.

Beatriz Christina Fernandez was born on February 22, 1964, in the city of San Juan on the island of Puerto Rico. "Gigi," an early childhood nickname, was given to her by her brothers, who had difficulty pronouncing "Beatriz." Her grandparents also lived in the Fernandez home and helped raise the four children, Carlos, Gabriel, Patricia, and Gigi. At four years old, she began to hit a tennis ball against a wall at the country club where her parents held memberships. Although her mother and father, Dr. Tuto and Beatriz Fernandez, both played tennis, they did not push or pressure Gigi into this sport. Young Gigi did not tire of her "wall tennis" and on her seventh birthday begged her parents for tennis lessons. She took lessons and practiced for hours every day, hitting against the wall. "I remember my first tennis match . . . I lost every game! I wasn't very good right away." By the time Gigi turned ten, she was ranked the number one junior player in all of Puerto Rico.

When Gigi began high school, she transferred to the Academia San Jose. She continued her ten-

"My proudest moment!" 1992 Olympics, Barcelona, Spain

nis, but it took a second seat to her social life. "When I switched schools I got a new set of friends and I got my driver's license. I just wanted to go out with my friends and be cool!" For almost a two-year period, Gigi changed her tennis schedule to lessons twice a week and practice three times a week for less than an hour each time. She played some tournaments on the weekends and was able to keep her top ranking. This enabled her to compete in the Pan American Games held in Puerto Rico in 1979, where she won a Bronze Medal in doubles tennis competition. In 1983, she traveled to Venezuela to represent Puerto Rico in the 1983 Pan American Games. Here, she was awarded two Silver Medals for singles and doubles tennis.

Looking back on her teen years, Gigi felt she should have been made to practice harder, so that she would have been better prepared to meet the challenge of professional competition and able to excel more quickly in the rankings. "There was good news and bad news about this time period. The bad news was I did not have to practice any harder. The good news was I kept winning and it kept me in tennis. This was a turning point for me and I could have very easily retired. I think if I had a boyfriend then, I would have quit tennis!"

During her eighteen years in San Juan, Gigi Fernandez did not aspire to become a professional tennis player. At that time, she remembers that tennis was not a popular sport in Puerto Rico and females were not encouraged or expected to choose a career in sports. She thought she would grow up, get married, have children, and dedicate her life to raising a family as her mother did.

In 1982, at the age of eighteen, Gigi Fernandez left home and entered Clemson University in South Carolina as a computer science major. She was awarded a full tennis scholarship, which paid all of her schooling expenses. In order to keep her scholarship, she was required to attend practice every day and to train with the tennis team. When she followed this routine, she became an improved player. By the end of her first year in college, she was the number two player on the team and had made the National Collegiate Athletic Association (NCAA) tennis finals. Her challenger in the finals was ranked twenty-seventh in the world and Gigi Fernandez, ranked about eightieth, was able to win match points. As a college freshman, winning all matches except for about three, almost convinced her to turn pro.

To help make the final decision to turn professional, Gigi Fernandez took the fall semester off to play tennis. She was successful in almost all of her matches and was able to beat the number ten player in the world. "It was a very difficult decision for me to turn pro. On the one hand, I had a free education and how many people really have this opportunity? When you turn pro it means that you accept money for playing tennis. You lose your college eligibility and amateur status. On the other hand, I knew I had a talent that was going to get me somewhere. Most girls turn pro at sixteen and I did not turn pro until I was nineteen. I was a late bloomer. School is important to me and it will always be there. I can go back to school when I retire from this sport, but I can only play tennis for so many years."

Early in her career, Gigi Fernandez emerged as a strong doubles tennis player. From the time she was twelve years old, she showed a natural instinct for this type of tennis. Usually, players are more successful in doubles matches when they are older and more mature. (In doubles competition there are two people playing together against two opponents.) Gigi Fernandez sees herself with a personality that is better suited to team play. She has been able to create the right "chemistry" with different partners to win major doubles tennis matches. Although she also competes in one-on-one singles matches, she is more successful in doubles. She has commented that it is difficult to excel in both singles and doubles tennis at the same time.

The amount of time Gigi Fernandez has spent on training has varied, beginning with an erratic schedule in Puerto Rico to a regular routine at Clemson. After turning pro, she began a year-round program that includes both physical and mental preparation at her home in Aspen, Colorado. Although the training and strategy improvement is centered on individual or singles competition, it also benefits the doubles game. Throughout the year, aerobic workouts, weight lifting, and footwork exercises called plyometrics help with building strength and stamina. During the summer months, she hikes, bikes, and runs. When there is snow on the ground, she does stair-step exercises and goes cross-country skiing. Her training coach also emphasizes proper nutrition and diet as part of her fitness program.

In any tennis competition, Gigi Fernandez must also come to the court mentally prepared to do her best and to keep focused during the game. Often, when opponents are closely matched in their physical abilities, the difference and the victory will depend on the player's mental toughness. To help her improve in this area, she works with a psychologist who specializes in sports psychology. "I learned how to visualize. If I have a match the next day, I visualize serving the ball and playing the game— and winning. So, when I actually play in the match, I've already done it in my mind, fifty times, and I don't feel panic. During the game I keep the same basic routines. I always bounce the ball three times before I serve and have a routine before I return a serve from the other player."

Gigi Fernandez's full training program equipped her for what she describes as the most exciting win of her career thus far. In 1992, she was selected as a member of the United States Olympic tennis team. Knowing her strength as a doubles player, she chose to play for the U.S. rather than Puerto Rico. Her only option playing for Puerto Rico was to play singles tennis and she felt that she had a better chance to win an Olympic medal in doubles.

The final gold medal game matched the U.S. doubles team against the top-ranked team from Spain. The Barcelona tennis stadium was filled with a cheering crowd waving signs and flags for their homeland's team. The winners of two out of three sets would determine the number one Olympic team in women's doubles tennis. The U.S. team won the first set of games. Then two events changed the momentum in the second set in favor of the Spanish team. Gigi Fernandez recalls that she was not able to serve the ball properly and began to lose points. Also during the second set, the King and Queen of Spain entered and remained to inspire their team on to victory. After the King and Queen arrived, the U.S. team lost six games in a row and the second set. Gigi Fernandez was able to regain her serving ability in the third set and, together with her partner, won the Gold Medal for the United States in an exciting finish.

Another memorable doubles game for Gigi Fernandez occurred in 1992. Just after competing in the U.S. Open, she was invited by then President George Bush to visit Camp David. "I played tennis with the President and his sons. The whole family was there, including the grandchildren. We all had lunch together—it was great. It was a thrill for me to have the President as my partner. We played against his two sons, George, Jr., and Neal, and the President and I won—we had to win!"

Playing in the French Open, June, 1993

After devoting the first ten years of her professional career to full-time tennis, Gigi has become involved in special programs working with children. "Up to this point in my career I have been very focused on tennis. I want to give something back, but it is hard to take time away from tennis. I feel I am approaching a stage in my career where I can expand and do more things."

One of the projects that Gigi Fernandez has undertaken is fund raising to help children with pediatric AIDS. She has participated in Pro-Am tennis tournaments where amateur athletes pay to play with professionals and has had her part of the proceeds donated to a center for pediatric AIDS victims. Another program she supports reaches about 10,000 children in Puerto Rico. Seventh through ninth graders from low-income areas are taught lessons in self-esteem, values in life, and the dangers of substance abuse. Once a year, all of these children go to a large coliseum for a special show with people who have achieved in entertainment, sports, or the arts. Gigi Fernandez has been promoting a yearly tennis exhibition, bringing professional players to Puerto Rico to help raise funds for the student self-esteem program.

To date, Gigi Fernandez is the only professional female athlete from Puerto Rico. She makes time to meet and work with young Puerto Rican girls to support their interest in tennis. "I am trying to help with the development of tennis in Puerto Rico. No other woman in Puerto Rico is earning a living

"Cross-country skiing with a backpack as part of my tennis training—not easy work!"

in sports. It's not for lack of talent, it's because girls are raised in a more traditional manner to take care of the home and family. But I don't think it has to be that way. So, I'm trying to make it okay in Puerto Rico for girls to become professional athletes." Gigi Fernandez hopes to start a mini-tennis camp for the top female players in Puerto Rico. In addition to working on improving their tennis skills, she will share her own experiences and teach them what it means to be a professional, how to train, and how to become disciplined.

To all children, Gigi Fernandez stresses the importance of having goals, dreams, and self-discipline. "Think about what you want to become in

Gigi with her three dogs at home in Aspen, Colorado

life. Imagine yourself as a professional baseball player or the CEO [Chief Executive Officer] of a company or whatever it is that you want to be. If there is something you want to achieve and you have a plan, then you must also have the discipline to implement it. With work, determination, discipline, and a plan, you can achieve any goal or dream in life."

For Gigi Fernandez, her goal and dream of being number one in both doubles and singles tennis motivates her to train. "It is not easy for me to work out. I do not like to practice and I never feel like getting on the stair-step machine to exercise when I am on the road. Especially when I am away from home, I have already been playing for two hours a day and am tired from the pressures and nerves of tournament play. The last thing I want to do is get on the stair-step machine, but I know training and exercise are important to be strong enough to reach my goal of winning—so I do it!"

Beginning in 1992, Gigi Fernandez started a string of victories that only one other women's doubles team has accomplished. There are many tennis tournaments played in several different countries throughout the year. Four are called "Grand Slam" events, considered by professional tennis players and the sporting world to be the most important: Wimbledon (England), the French Open, the Australian Open, and the U.S. Open. When a doubles team or singles tennis player wins all four in the same year, they have achieved a

Grand Slam. Gigi Fernandez won six consecutive Grand Slam events spanning the 1992 and 1993 seasons and came within one match of achieving a Grand Slam in 1993. Although winning six consecutive Grand Slam events is a great accomplishment, Gigi still needs to win four Grand Slam matches in the same year to earn the title.

Gigi Fernandez travels about forty weeks a year playing in the major tennis tournaments around the world. When she is not on tour, she is at home in Aspen, Colorado, training and winding down from being on the road. She has three dogs, a golden retriever, a Pomeranian, and a "mutt," who help her train by going with her on long hikes. Her brothers and sister and their families live in Puerto Rico. When Gigi was in her late twenties, her parents divorced and moved to two different locations in the United States. During any free time at home or at tennis tournaments, Gigi Fernandez enjoys reading or working on her computer. Describing herself as a "computer nerd," she takes her computer with her whenever she travels. She belongs to a computer information network that she can access from anywhere in the world through a phone modem.

Following her own advice, Gigi Fernandez pursues her goals with hard work and determination. She has seized opportunities that tennis has brought her way to travel around the world, meet different people, teach others, and to fulfill her dreams.

Andy Garcia

—The severed hand that had been found in the garbage dump was carefuly examined by Homicide Detective John Berlin
—An unlikely hero took credit for rescuing victims from a burning plane crash
—Remarkable math test scores achieved at a formerly unremarkable high school were questioned by suspicious officials, including Dr. Ramirez
—Vincent Mancini's father, Sonny Corleone, was gunned down at a toll booth years earlier, and Vincent seemed destined to be the family Godfather

Those were some of his movie roles, but the real Andy Garcia chatted with television host David Letterman about his upcoming documentary on a legendary Cuban musician.

Andy Garcia played a newspaper reporter in Dead Again, *1991.*

Andy Garcia is an actor who delights in playing different characters. Even as he began his career, often with minor parts, he attracted the attention of audiences, reviewers, and the Hollywood community. As a producer and director, Mr. Garcia wants to share his Cuban heritage and its music, both very much a part of his life. He spent his first five years in Cuba, before his family fled the Castro regime.

When Andres Arturo Garcia Menendez was born in Havana on April 12, 1956, his family had a very comfortable life. His father was a lawyer, as well as a farmer with a successful produce business. The "Garcia Number One" is a type of avocado that he developed. Andy's mother was an English teacher, although young Andy did not learn English before coming to the United States. When Andy was born, his brother was three, and his sister was five.

In 1959, Fidel Castro came to power in Cuba. Life on the island changed rapidly. The new government began to nationalize banks and take private property. Andy says that his father got particularly upset upon hearing that his children would be educated in the ways of the revolutionary government. The Garcias left Cuba soon after the Bay of Pigs invasion, an unsuccessful try by Cuban exiles to overthrow Castro in 1961. First, Mrs. Garcia and their three children flew to Miami, Florida. Mr. Garcia joined his family there several months later.

Andy says that his family did not come to the U.S. as immigrants wanting to fulfill the "American Dream." Instead, like many other Cubans who fled, they were political exiles, in Miami only until Cuba was free again. However, Castro stayed in control and Andy grew up in Miami. He remembers very little of Cuba and regrets not being able to grow up in Havana without Castro.

Life in Miami Beach was very different for the Garcia family. They did not have the money or status which they had in Cuba. Mrs. Garcia was a secretary. Mr. Garcia could not practice law in the United States, and he did not have his land. Eventually, he was able to build a successful perfume business, but at first he worked for a caterer. Andy has remarked that in those days they were quite poor, but would always eat well. For extra change, Andy picked up empty soft drink bottles from the beach and the streets.

Adjustment was particularly difficult for the Garcia boys, who did not speak English. At first, Andy was involved in many fistfights, often because he did not understand what was being said to him. Also, Andy says he felt isolated while he was struggling to learn English.

When Andy was a student at Miami Beach Senior High, he had a very busy life and tight schedule. After school and basketball practice, he took a bus to downtown Miami. There, he had a job sweeping the warehouse floors in the hosiery company where his father worked at the time.

Andy enjoyed playing sports, including football and baseball, with basketball as his favorite. He says that he would have become a professional basketball player if possible, but he was considered too short for college basketball. Also, he was physically weakened after having an illness called mononucleosis.

Socially, Andy enjoyed discos with a crowd that included his brother. Andy was not the usual younger brother who just tagged along, however. His brother has recalled that Andy actually attracted girls, since he played the bongo drums and piano. Another of his musical interests was collecting old records of Cuban singers and bands.

Andy Garcia started college at nearby Florida International University. He was not sure what he wanted to study, but auditioned for a play. His first performance was at a Miami Beach community center. He found that he loved acting. He took it very seriously and realized that this would be his profession. In 1977, Andy left school, but not before he had met a photography student who would later become his wife. She had also fled Cuba with her family.

Andy began his career with regional theater in Florida and with jobs in the Dominican Republic and Puerto Rico. However, he knew that his best chances would be in Los Angeles. In 1978, he moved to the Hollywood section of that city, but acting jobs did not come easily. Andy recalls one agent who would not represent him unless he changed his looks and eliminated his Spanish accent. He lost his chance at one role because the person interviewing him thought he did not appear ethnic enough. Andy often felt rejected, but did not compromise or give up. To support himself, he worked as a waiter and on loading docks.

In 1980, Andy was noticed by a casting agent while he was with an improvisational group, which created as it performed, at the Comedy Store in Los Angeles. Finally, in 1981, he had his first television part, as a gang member in the pilot episode of "Hill Street Blues."

Other television and movie work followed. Often, Mr. Garcia played either a law breaker or law enforcer. His roles at the time were rather small, but he created memorable characters and stole scenes. In *The Mean Season* (1985), he was a detective. He played a very convincing drug dealer in *Eight Million Ways to Die* (1986). After that, the producers planning *The Untouchables* were eager to have him play one of Al Capone's gangsters in that film. However, Andy preferred to be one of the lawmen determined to crush Capone, and he was. In *Stand and Deliver* (1988), Andy Garcia was an enforcer of another type. He was Dr. Ramirez, one of the officials to question the extraordinary Advanced Placement math test scores earned by teacher Jaime Escalante's students. After playing another policeman in *Black Rain* (1989), Andy Garcia became Investigator Raymond Avilla, who was assigned to uncover the truth about a fellow officer in *Internal Affairs* (1990). This marked the first time Mr. Garcia's name appeared above the title of a film.

The Untouchables, Black Rain, and *Internal Affairs* were all Paramount films, and that same studio was about to start *The Godfather Part III,* to be directed by Francis Ford Coppola. The studio recommended Mr. Garcia for a part, but Mr. Coppola wanted to rely on screen tests. Andy won the role of Vincent Mancini. As Vincent committed crimes and won hearts, Andy Garcia earned an Oscar nomination for best supporting actor.

Though Andy Garcia's career developed around many violent and volatile characters, his personal life was just the opposite. In 1982, he and his wife were married. As Mr. Garcia gathered honors and rave reviews, he and his family lived quietly in a suburban San Fernando Valley home in Los Angeles. When on location for a film, he would call home frequently. Bongo rhythms were heard from his dressing room trailer as he played in his spare time. He also enjoyed golf and the family dogs.

In 1992, Andy Garcia worked on several very different projects. For *Jennifer Eight,* he played yet another policeman, John Berlin. Even without the victim's entire body, he discovered a critical clue on the fingertips of her detached hand. The suspense intensified as Investigator Berlin himself became a murder suspect. In a complete departure from most of his other roles, Mr. Garcia was an opportunist in the comedy *Hero*. He wrongly took credit and rewards for saving lives, then used his newly found fame for good deeds.

As *Jennifer Eight* and *Hero* were being made, Andy Garcia was creating two films of his own. Both would reflect his enthusiasm for Cuban culture and music. He produced and directed a documentary in Spanish on the influential Cuban musician, Israel "Cachao" Lopez. Mr. Lopez was one of the creators of mambo dance music in the 1930s. Mr. Garcia appeared with Mr. Lopez at the film's premiere in Miami in February, 1993. He hopes that more people will learn about Cuban music and Mr. Lopez's contributions. Noting the importance of classical Cuban music, he says it should be taught in schools. Also, it helps pass down Cuban culture. On a personal level, Mr. Garcia feels that Cuban music is a link to a homeland he hardly remembers.

When the documentary debuted, Andy Garcia was still preparing *The Lost City*, which would recall Havana of the 1950s and be a film that Mr. Garcia would produce, direct, and star in. He commissioned noted Cuban writer Guillermo Cabrera Infante to create the screenplay. The movie would feature the music of Israel Lopez and his orchestra.

Andy Garcia has not returned to his birthplace since he was uprooted at the age of five. He would like to go back one day, but only when Cuba is free of Castro's rule. Mr. Garcia maintains close ties with many of his old friends and the Cuban-

Andy Garcia in a publicity photo for Jennifer Eight

American community in the Miami area. He and his family have homes in both Miami, Florida, and Los Angeles.

Andy was also in Florida to help after the destruction of Hurricane Andrew. Soon after the storm struck Homestead, he arrived with a forty-foot truck to distribute needed items to the devastated victims. He approached Gloria and Emilio Estefan about organizing a benefit concert, and learned that one had already been planned. Andy participated, as did numerous other stars, and helped raise money for the recovery.

In addition to receiving an Oscar nomination, Mr. Garcia has also been honored by Nosotros, an organization concerned with Hispanics in the entertainment industry and improving the portrayal of Hispanics. Andy Garcia was selected as "Star of the Year" in 1991 by the National Association of Theater Owners. In August, 1992, he received a Desi Entertainment Award along with other entertainers, including Gloria Estefan, Edward James Olmos, and Celia Cruz.

Mr. Garcia says that his children do not think of him as a movie star, although they know he is an actor. They have not seen many of his films, however, because he feels that they are too young for the themes and violence of some of his work.

On screen, Andy Garcia is very convincing as a hardened killer or zealous policeman. He truly enjoys acting and creating roles, while he remains devoted to his family, culture, and music. Seated across from David Letterman on his television show, he discussed some of his films, his background, and faint memories of Cuba. Then the talk shifted readily to music, and Andy introduced Israel "Cachao" Lopez and several other musicians. Quite happily, Andy Garcia ended his segment with Cuban music, as he joined the group and played the bongos.

Roberto C. Goizueta

If selling soft drinks made the most money for your company and you wanted to expand, what would you do? If selling in foreign countries was more profitable than in the United States, where would you look for sales growth? If thirsty consumers in the U.S. already drank an average of nearly three hundred servings per person per year, but the average in China, the world's most populated country, was not even one glass per year, and your company had recently resumed business in India, the second-most populated country, would you see these areas as waiting markets for your beverages? If a new product failed, how would you recover?

These questions are not word problems to be worked during a math test, but real-life business decisions which were tackled by Roberto Crispulo Goizueta, the Chairman and Chief Executive Officer of The Coca-Cola Company. Mr. Goizueta's leadership and decisions have made billions of dollars for the shareowners of the company, and he has been rewarded for a job well-done.

Mr. Goizueta has dedicated most of his life to Coca-Cola, working there since 1954. In fact, the only other job he has held was with his family's businesses, and that was only for his first year after college.

Sugar and sugar products were an important part of Roberto Goizueta's background as he grew up in Cuba. During the 1700s, Cuba became known for its sugarcane. Increasingly, much of the Cuban economy depended on its sugar industry, which became highly mechanized. By the mid-1800s, the island provided almost one-third of all the sugar in the world. In the late 1800s, Roberto's grandfathers came from Spain and settled in Cuba. His mother's father founded a sugar business, which his own father, Crispulo, continued.

Roberto was born in Havana, the capital of Cuba, on November 18, 1931, the son of Crispulo Goizueta and Aida Cantera de Goizueta. His family had sugarcane plantations as well as a mill and a refinery. Crispulo Goizueta received education in the United States, and so did Roberto. After the Colegio de Belen in Cuba, sixteen-year-old Roberto left for Cheshire Academy, a prep school in Connecticut. At first, he knew little English, but he has said he learned with the help of a dictionary and seeing the same movies many times. Another trick he used when he did not completely understand the language was to actually memorize portions of textbooks. At Yale University, also in Connecticut, he majored in chemical engineering. He graduated from Yale in 1953, and in June of that same year, he married Olga Casteleiro, also from Havana. They had known each other for a long time, and they dated while both were studying in the U.S.

Roberto started his career with the family sugar business in Cuba, but decided to try a different course and work for a large company. One reason he gave was wanting to prove himself independently. With his father's permission, Roberto answered an ad he saw in a newspaper for a bilingual chemical engineer. In 1954, Roberto Goizueta went to work as a quality control chemist for Coca-Cola in Cuba. In December of that same year his son, Roberto Segundo Goizueta, was born.

During his early years at Coca-Cola, Mr. Goizueta worked at the Havana bottling plant. He rose to Coca-Cola's chief technical position in Cuba. Roberto and his father discussed purchasing bottling plants. With money loaned by his father, who greatly believed in business ownership, he bought one hundred shares of Coca-Cola stock. By buying stock, Roberto would own at least a small fraction of the company. Mr. Goizueta imagines that if life in Cuba had stayed the same, his family would

Roberto C. Goizueta, Chairman and CEO of The Coca-Cola Company

have bought the bottling franchise in Havana and he would have remained there himself and become a Coca-Cola bottler.

However, life did not remain the same in Cuba after Fidel Castro took control in 1959. His government began to seize private property and radically change the country economically and politically. Hundreds of thousands of Cubans fled, especially the well-educated, professional, and affluent. In 1961, Roberto and his family, which now included three children, Roberto S., Olga, and Javier, were allowed to leave Cuba, but their family possessions had to remain behind. Mr. Goizueta arrived in Miami with just twenty dollars, but he knew he had a job with Coca-Cola and he also fully expected to return to Havana very soon. He was certainly correct about his future with The Coca-Cola Company, but not about his own or the company's future in Havana. Very soon, Coca-Cola facilities in Cuba were taken over by Castro's government and nationalized. The Goizuetas settled in the U.S. as refugees. Roberto never became the bottler in Havana, and Coca-Cola is not even sold in Cuba, but he did continue his rising career with the company.

For several years, Mr. Goizueta commuted from Miami to the Bahamas, where he was working as an assistant to the vice-president who supervised Coca-Cola in Latin America. In 1964, he moved to Atlanta, Georgia, company headquarters. For two years, he was an assistant to the vice-president of research and development, and then in 1966, he was promoted to vice-president of engineering, with responsibility for research and quality. He was thirty-five and the youngest vice-president at Coca-Cola.

In 1969, Mr. Goizueta became a citizen of the

United States. During the 1970s, his career steadily advanced, as he was named one of six vice-chairmen in 1979. In 1980, he became president and chief operating officer, as well as a director of the company. Mr. Goizueta was certainly not the only non-U.S.-born executive at Coca-Cola headquarters, as others hailed from countries such as Argentina, Germany, and Egypt. Historically, the upper ranks of Coca-Cola management had been filled with Georgians, but increasingly, the company picked leaders with experience in its growing international business. Yet when Roberto Goizueta was named Chairman of the Board and Chief Executive Officer (CEO), he was the first non-Georgian to head the company.

Coca-Cola itself was born in the state of Georgia in the 1880s, after a pharmacist named John Pemberton perfected his formula for a particular syrup he had created in a kettle in his backyard. Initially, Coca-Cola was sold only as a syrup, to be mixed with carbonated water at a drugstore soda fountain. Then, two businessmen bought the right to bottle Coca-Cola in most of the country. Supposedly, they got the idea for bottling the beverage after noticing people drinking from bottles in Cuba. Over the years, a huge network of bottlers would grow, as exclusive rights to bottle and sell the beverage in specific areas were sold. In the meantime, the formula for Coca-Cola, handwritten by Dr. Pemberton, was locked in an Atlanta bank vault. Coca-Cola would become a symbol of the U.S. By the turn of the century, it was sold in all the states and territories. During the late 1920s, under company head Robert Woodruff, sales in Europe began. During World War II, Mr. Woodruff and the company strived to have Coca-Cola available to U.S. armed forces, no matter how far from home they were. The U.S. government even helped to set up some foreign bottling plants, realizing how important Coke was to wartime morale.

When Roberto Goizueta became Chairman and CEO in March, 1981, he knew there were important decisions to be made. Mr. Woodruff had not been head of the company for many years, but he was still very influential. He and Mr. Goizueta admired each other greatly, and until Mr. Woodruff's death in 1985, Mr. Goizueta visited and consulted with him regularly. Mr. Goizueta has also worked closely with the president of Coca-Cola and other company executives.

In March, 1981, Mr. Goizueta announced that the company would take more risks, and prophetically, said that if a decision proved wrong, another decision could be made to correct it. During the first few years of his chairmanship, Coca-Cola changed several of its long-standing business practices. While the company had other beverages such as Sprite, Tab, and Minute Maid juices, there was only one drink with the name of Coca-Cola until 1982. In that year, diet Coke was introduced. Other varieties such as Caffeine Free and cherry Coke would follow. For decades, there had been a

Mr. Goizueta at the Varsity, a popular drive-in restaurant in Atlanta, during a Coca-Cola "Customer Appreciation Week" visit. Some schoolchildren, also there at the time, received souvenir Coca-Cola pins and Varsity hats.

belief that the company should not be in debt, but Mr. Goizueta thought borrowing and investing more in the company would be profitable. Also, the percentage of company earnings paid to stockholders, known as dividends, was lowered to leave more money for the company to invest in the Coca-Cola system. The company bought all or portions of a number of bottling operations, giving Coca-Cola a stronger voice in the bottling and distribution of its products. This investment, in turn, increased the value of the company and the value of each shareowner's stock. For awhile, the company was diversifying, and it bought Columbia Pictures in 1982.

Perhaps Roberto Goizueta's most famous decision involved the introduction of new Coke in April, 1985. Coca-Cola had been losing consumers to Pepsi, and taste tests showed a newly formulated Coke was preferred to actual Coca-Cola. With much fanfare, the old product was abandoned and new Coke was launched into the market to better compete with Pepsi. Almost immediately, Coca-Cola heard from its customers, but reaction was not positive. Many people were outraged that their old beverage was no longer available. Mr. Goizueta soon realized that replacing familiar Coke with new Coke was a mistake, and he quickly took his own advice by making another decision to correct the first. Just three months after its replacement, the old Coca-Cola was returned to the shelves, relabeled as Coca-Cola Classic. The enormous publicity boosted sales and, happily for Mr. Goizueta, Coca-Cola increased in popularity.

Mr. Goizueta closely watches the giant company and continuously makes decisions aimed at enriching its stockholders. By 1990, strategy had changed from diversifying into other businesses, such as entertainment, to concentrating on soft drinks. Columbia Pictures was sold in 1989. The bottling system has been restructured, and the company has financial interest in many bottlers all over the world.

Coca-Cola is sold in over 195 countries, and the company increasingly looks abroad for expanded sales. It makes more profit on selling its concentrate in foreign countries. Also, it would like the billions of people around the world, including those in the two most populated countries of China and India, to drink as much Coca-Cola per person as those in the U.S. do. Often, doing business in foreign countries involves politics and foreign government approvals. When Mr. Goizueta visited Poland in early 1993, his discussions with Polish Prime Minister Hanna Suchocka ranged from pending laws to when the diet version of Coke would be available in her country. Mr. Goizueta is known for his attention to detail, whether on a foreign trip or poring over company charts.

Investors have been rewarded by seeing the worth of the company climb. During the first twelve years that Mr. Goizueta was chairman, the value of Coca-Cola increased from $4.3 billion to around $56 billion, and the value of its stock soared. The first one hundred shares of stock he bought with $8,000 borrowed from his father have split many times over the nearly forty years he has owned them. Just that one investment multiplied into 28,800 shares, worth over $1 million by mid-1993.

Roberto Goizueta works very hard for the company, with most of his time devoted to business, but he also has an active civic and family life. As one of the most prominent corporate leaders in the country, he was asked to attend the economic conference held by President Bill Clinton just weeks after Mr. Clinton was elected. Mr. Goizueta has also served on many boards of directors, including the Ford Motor Company, Eastman Kodak, and the Trust Company of Georgia, where the handwritten Coca-Cola recipe still lies in a vault. He is also a board member of the Boys & Girls Clubs of America and a Trustee of Emory University.

Most years, Mr. Goizueta has limited his vacation to only one week, usually renting a house on Sea Island off the coast of Georgia. He and his wife enjoy golfing together and going to Atlanta Symphony Orchestra concerts. Mr. Goizueta is also a fan of country music, particularly Randy Travis.

The eldest Goizueta son, Roberto S., has his doctorate in theology and teaches at Loyola University in Chicago. Daughter Olga is an attorney, and Javier has worked in corporate business. Mr. and Mrs. Goizueta have seven grandchildren who frequently visit, and in 1987 they moved to a larger home with more room. Until then, Mr. Goizueta and his wife chose to live in the same two-story, four-bedroom house they bought in 1964 when they first moved to Atlanta. Mr. Goizueta remarked that it was comfortable enough at the time, and, after losing an enormous home and wealth in Cuba, he appreciated other aspects of life differently.

Mr. Goizueta derives great pleasure from his family, his achievements for The Coca-Cola Company, and its challenges, and he takes seriously his role to make the shareholders richer. He says that he thinks of how to improve the company almost constantly. He said that he even thought about business while shaving, then added that he thought he would be safe because he used an electric razor. Even when he arises each morning at 5:30 A.M., Roberto Goizueta is thinking about where to expand, how to increase profits, and the best way to get more people to drink more Coca-Cola products.

Carolina Herrera

Maria Carolina Josefina Pacanins y Nino and her three sisters were daughters of Guillermo Pacanins Acevedo, an important figure in Venezuelan aviation who became governor of Caracas, and Maria Cristina Nino de Pacanins, a fashionable society woman. Their large, tile-roofed house in Caracas stretched amidst fragrant tropical gardens, and there were trips to cities such as New York and Paris. The prominent and wealthy family had a long history in Venezuela. The girls were expected to follow tradition, with marriage and children.

In many ways, Carolina has conformed precisely. Today, she is married and has four daughters and three grandsons. She is well-traveled, and knows Spanish, English, and French. She is elegantly dressed, does charity work, and has homes in Caracas and New York. However, she also has an extraordinarily successful career, which was not anticipated. She used her talent for designing clothes and entered the working end of the fashion world when she was already in her forties. Her company, Carolina Herrera, Ltd., has since grown in size and influence, and she adores this new aspect of her life.

"In my family, all the women were well-dressed" is Carolina's way of describing how she learned about fashion. She had no formal training in design, but even from her early years she was exposed to the best designers, the women who wore such clothes, and the glamorous lives they led.

"I come from a very old family, in Venezuela for many centuries. Mine is an old, colonial Spanish family." Native cultures lived in the land now known as Venezuela before Christopher Columbus arrived in 1498. Spanish settlers followed, including Carolina's ancestors, and added to the population. Venezuela was under Spanish rule until 1821, and later became an independent republic. Carolina's family stayed and was active in Venezuelan politics.

Carolina was born on January 8, 1939, in Caracas. Her father had a long career of service to his country. He was educated at a school of military aviation and rose to a high rank in the Venezuelan Air Force. Carolina notes he was also "a pioneer of commercial aviation in Venezuela." In addition, he was the governor of Caracas in the early 1950s. Another side of Carolina's father was his interest in race horses, which he kept and bred. In his later years, he was retired and wrote on the history of aviation in Venezuela. He died in June, 1992.

Carolina's mother "was artistic and wrote well. She and her sister were good at music and painting." Carolina traveled to France from the time she was a little girl. Her mother and grandmother bought clothes in Paris. She recalls long waits as her grandmother was fitted for hats. During a trip when she was thirteen, her grandmother introduced her to the famous designer Balenciaga, "but I did not think about designing," she adds. Sadly, Carolina's mother died before Carolina became a famous designer herself.

When asked about her favorites while growing up, Carolina first mentions sports, riding and tennis. She quickly follows with horses and dogs, saying that she used to show dogs and how they take a long time to train. When discussing school, she admits that she was not a very good student, particularly in math, but says she loved history.

In the Pacanins family, there was much discipline and order. Carolina and her sisters were taught to look and behave with a certain grace. At times, Carolina tired of looking proper and innocent. She wanted to wear a red dress to her first Venezuelan society ball, but her parents would not let her. Instead, she wore a flowing, white gown. Within bounds, she was permitted to experiment a

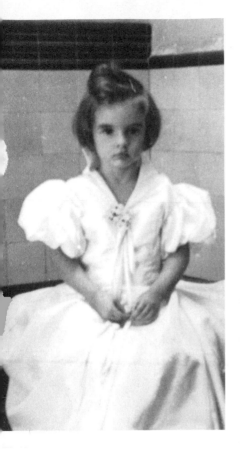

Carolina at the age of four
in Caracas, Venezuela

Sixteen-year-old Carolina
at a dog show in
Caracas, Venezuela

bit with fashion. Increasingly, she enjoyed creating her own look, while she also wore designs by others. These early years would provide experience and inspiration for her career, still decades and a continent away. Even the scent of jasmine, from the garden next to her childhood bedroom, would become part of her future company. Yet, back in 1957, Carolina thought nothing of a career. She married her first husband at eighteen and had two daughters, Mercedes and Ana Luisa, but the marriage ended.

On September 20, 1968, Carolina married Reinaldo Herrera. Her wedding dress, with an open collar and a hemline just above her knees, was her own design. She and Reinaldo had known one another for years. He was also from a distinguished Venezuelan family, whose home was Caracas' noted mansion, Hacienda La Vega, built in 1590. The Herreras enjoyed their new life together, and traveled often to New York and Europe. Two daughters were born, Carolina, Jr. and Patricia. Reinaldo, Carolina, and all four girls resided at La Vega.

During this time, Carolina had been selecting her wardrobe from world-famous designers as well as designing for herself. "I could envision proportions and colors, and worked with seamstresses in making clothes. I did not know how to make patterns or cut fabric, but I would have an idea and direct." She also designed for some friends.

Carolina had a fulfilling family life, the luxury of both La Vega and exciting foreign trips. She had already been on the International Best Dressed List for many years. She was active socially, wearing her gowns to many affairs. As more people noticed her clothes, she became encouraged to create a line of her own, not just for friends, but to actually show and sell. Carolina had never considered a career, but she felt prepared to try design and decided to test her talent. Quite suddenly, she was competing against legendary names.

Carolina started work with one seamstress. She wanted to present her clothes in New York City, feeling that success there could launch her career. "I had great luck. I wanted to design and show to store buyers. There was no company, just a big collection of twenty dresses, coats, suits, and evening wear. They wanted to buy! What should I do? I went back to Venezuela and found a partner who is still there, Armando de Armas. He is not in fashion, but owns the biggest publishing company in Venezuela and Miami. I came back to New York, put together the company, and had my first show. The stores started buying immediately!"

This first show was marked by large sleeves. Mrs. Herrera explained that when women sit at a table, what is seen is only from the waist up, so sleeves deserve special attention. Her clothes included suits for luncheons, a silk outfit for poolside, and elegant gowns. Mrs. Herrera knew what her clients did and what they wanted. That same year, 1981, she was elected to the Best Dressed Hall of Fame.

Mrs. Herrera never dreamed that her new com-

Mrs. Herrera using a dress form to work with a design

pany, Carolina Herrera, Ltd., would be such an instant success, nor that it would involve so much. She had planned to travel from Caracas to New York when necessary for her business, but found she was needed in Manhattan full-time. She moved there in 1980, but has remained a Venezuelan citizen. "I had no difficulty in adjusting to life in New York because I had been in and out of the city all the time. In 1982, my children came. They had no difficulties in language or schooling because they also knew English, having gone to a British school in Caracas." The Herreras continued their active social life, but for Carolina there was now a greater purpose in noticing what everyone wore.

Carolina Herrera, Ltd. is still in New York and has grown over the years. "I am president of the company and take care of creativity. I am informed of management and business figures, and public relations, but those are separate. I do not think a designer can do all. There are ninety-five employees, all in New York. The clothes are made in New York. That works better, for control." She says her job involves "constant research, which requires an open eye in the world. Everyday, I learn something new. I see and experience shapes and materials. Fashion is ephemeral. It does not last and has to change all the time, an evolution of ideas. Like a laboratory, there is research and experimentation."

Carolina Herrera's ideas become fashion after many steps. "First I buy the materials, and from them I get inspiration. Depending on the season, I decide how many suits and coats to design, for example. I work on a sample collection, for the reviews and buyers." Sometimes these fashion shows can be giant extravaganzas, but for her Fall, 1993, collection, Mrs. Herrera tried a series of many smaller shows over a two-week period. She explains that for a show, "Each item is only made in one size, to fit the model. For the styles that are picked, patterns are made and graded for sizes. They must fit to perfection and be of very fine assembly. Then, they are delivered to stores." Samples for the shows are ready about six months after the fabric is first ordered, and then the styles are in the stores six months after that. The entire process takes about a year.

Carolina Herrera's clothes are known for their elegance, and that word is often repeated in newspaper reviews of her fashion shows. The garments have simple lines rather than many distracting details. Fine fabrics, such as silk, velvet, and chiffon are used. Her attention to sleeves and padded shoulders has remained a hallmark. She has also favored black-and-white polka dots. Her company even packaged her signature perfume, which incorporated the jasmine of her childhood, in a polka-dotted box. Over the years, the company has expanded its offerings to some less expensive and more casual clothes, a bridal collection, a men's fragrance, and jewelry. "Eyewear, handbags, shoes, and stockings are recent. There is always something else. It is important to have licenses," says Mrs. Herrera, but she cautions, "It is important to be careful."

Women pay high prices for Carolina Herrera's designs, and she wants them to be very satisfied. "For me, fit is most important. When women are pleased with how a dress fits, they will come back and buy more. If clothes do not fit properly, they will not come back." She may have originally designed clothes for social functions like the ones she would attend. However, her experiences and appeal have broadened, and she thinks that women at work can also wear some of her styles. Now, whether on the job or socially, Mrs. Herrera will only wear clothes that she herself has designed.

Carolina Herrera has earned some very famous clients. Former First Lady Nancy Reagan and Britain's Princess Margaret have worn her evening dresses. Another former First Lady, Jacqueline Kennedy Onassis, was said to consider Mrs. Herrera a favorite designer. Mrs. Onassis' daughter, Caroline Kennedy Schlossberg, wore a wedding gown by Mrs. Herrera. Plans for that wedding were closely guarded, and there was much guessing about the invitations, the menu, who would be in the bridal party, and, of course, the gown. Initially, it was merely rumored to be by Mrs. Herrera. When that was confirmed, speculation then focused on the design and fabric. Mrs. Herrera's office did its best to keep the details a secret. Finally, on July 19, 1986, the wedding day, the world saw the floor-length, white silk organza bridal gown.

The sleeves were gathered for Mrs. Herrera's broad-shouldered look. Mr. and Mrs. Herrera were among the wedding guests.

Carolina Herrera enjoys sharing in a bride's plans for her wedding and designing the gown. She has remarked that it is often easier when a bride comes by herself, without her mother. Mrs. Herrera was forced to keep her opinions to herself when her second daughter, Ana Luisa, was married in October, 1989. Ana Luisa wanted her mother to design her bridal gown, but she had definite ideas about what she wanted. Mrs. Herrera did her best to create the dress without interfering. The result was a large skirt covered with tulle. Missing were the broad shoulders.

So far, Ana Luisa is the only one of Mrs. Herrera's daughters who is truly interested in fashion and has pursued it in her career. She works as a fashion editor for *Mademoiselle* and lives in New York. Her older sister, Mercedes, lives with her husband and three sons in Venezuela. Mrs. Herrera visits and spends every August with her grandsons. The third daughter, Carolina Herrera, Jr., graduated from Vassar in 1992, after studying bio-psychology. Mrs. Herrera mentions Carolina, Jr.'s interest in medical school. Carolina, Jr., has appeared as a model for her mother and owns some clothes designed by her, but on campus she more

Carolina Herrera with her husband, Reinaldo Herrera, in their New York City home

often wore jeans and T-shirts. Patricia, the youngest, started Brown University in the fall of 1992, fond of history and literature.

When asked about her most gratifying accomplishment, Mrs. Herrera does not hesitate in answering, "My children!" She then adds, "For what I have done in twelve years, I am grateful. I started with a small company and it has grown." Crediting habits instilled during her early years, she says, "I am very well organized and disciplined. That is very important so that I find time for everything." She admits that her career has changed her life, that she is not as free. She has also sacrificed privacy, noting how she was a reserved person but was regularly forced to talk about herself and make professional appearances as part of her business. However, Mrs. Herrera believes a real key to her success and happiness is her ability to finish after a long day and not take her work home with her. She says that she has always put her family first. The Herrera family continues to live in New York, where Mr. Herrera is an editor at *Vanity Fair*.

When mentioning leisure time, Carolina Herrera says, "I now enjoy staying in the house and not going out. I used to do a lot, but not anymore. I like small dinners, perhaps eight to ten people. I enjoy movies, concerts, opera, and walking in the park. It all depends on my mood and the weather." She is also involved with community and charity organizations. She works for causes such as those that support research on cancer and AIDS.

Carolina Herrera enjoys the career she never thought she would have. She walks to work with her black poodle, Alfonso, who stays with her at the office. "Every day is different. That is why it is so much fun. My job involves creativity, thoughts, and lots of excitement!"

Lourdes Lopez

The teacher gave the students an assignment to select a job and, with the salary earned each month, to plan a budget that would pay for a place to live, food, clothing, and any other living expenses. Lourdes Lopez already knew what career she would choose to research—ballerina. "I went to the library, opened up an encyclopedia, and looked up ballet. There were six companies in the United States jam-packed with dancers working year-round. Their salaries were quoted there. And I went, 'Wow! I can do this! I can go to New York. I can do this for a living. I can actually grow up to be what I want to be!' It was very exciting information for me at the time."

Lourdes Lopez has been a Principal Dancer with the New York City Ballet since 1984. She joined the ballet company just after turning sixteen. Beginning as a member of the corps, she was promoted to the rank of Soloist in 1981 and then became a Principal Dancer. She has danced many leading roles, as well as created dance roles in a variety of ballet performances. Lourdes Lopez has also appeared on the PBS television series, "Dance in America." Perhaps the most unusual credit to her career was to attract the attention of "Chip" and Louise Landry, ballet enthusiasts and racehorse owners. They named one of their thoroughbreds Lourdes Lopez, after their favorite ballerina.

The youngest of three girls, Lourdes Lopez was born to Felix and Marta Lopez on May 2, 1958, in Havana, Cuba. About a year later, posing as tourists to the United States, Marta Lopez and her daughters fled from Cuba at the outset of Fidel Castro's regime. Felix, a former officer in the army which opposed Castro and his supporters, joined his family about two weeks later and they settled in Miami, Florida. Here, Lourdes and her two sisters, Terry and Barbara, went to public schools.

At the time Lourdes began kindergarten at Coral Way Elementary School, there was a large influx of Spanish-speaking children to the Miami area from Cuba. One of the first bilingual education programs was started in the school she attended. Lourdes and her classmates studied all the subjects in English for the first half of the day, changed classrooms, and then studied the same subjects in Spanish in the afternoon. She participated in this program until eighth grade and felt it to be helpful. "My first language was Spanish and that's what I spoke at home. English-speaking students were speaking Spanish as fluently as I was, with no accent whatsoever. And Spanish-speaking students were able to speak English just as fluently. I grew up in an environment where I felt at home speaking English or speaking Spanish. I didn't feel like the odd person out. It's a great opportunity to learn another language as a child. Unfortunately, it's something you don't always appreciate until you are much older."

Lourdes Lopez's love for ballet began at a very young age. She remembers her mother telling her about how she was always cutting out ballerina paper dolls. After turning five years old, she developed orthopedic problems with her legs and had to wear corrective shoes. When her mother took her to buy the special shoes, she instead tried on all the ballet pointe shoes which were also on display. When the special shoes were no longer needed, the doctor felt that dance exercises would help to further strengthen her legs. She and her sister, Terry, began to take a children's ballet class after school once a week.

At eight-and-a-half-years old, Lourdes Lopez changed ballet studios. Her sister stopped taking lessons and her mother would continue the costly lessons only if Lourdes was serious about ballet. Lourdes did not want to stop, and with her new Russian teacher, Alexander Nigodoff, the formal

Lourdes Lopez in the ballet Apollo, *choreographed by George Balanchine*

ballet training began. She was required to take ballet classes every day after school, and also on Saturdays.

"Alexander Nigodoff was the one who really opened up the ballet world to me—the mystery of it. He was the one who taught me the names for the different ballet steps. He told me there were story ballets like *Cinderella, Sleeping Beauty, Swan Lake*. He introduced me to the music of these ballets and how to count and add steps to the musical phrases. He showed me exercises that I would need to do every day to perform these ballets."

By the time she was ten years old, Lourdes Lopez had been to New York to audition for the Joffrey School and the School of American Ballet. She was offered scholarships by both schools and chose the School of American Ballet scholarship to continue her dance studies in Miami. Ballet classes were daily, six days a week, after school and on Saturday mornings. Sundays were spent catching up on school work. During the summers, she would take dance classes, too. Her schedule was very different from her group of friends, who were involved in school activities and traveled to many places on summer vacations. As a result, she often felt left out or out of place and that her friends did not quite understand her love or dedication to dance.

In the eighth grade, an event occurred that gave Lourdes Lopez a chance to show her friends the reason for spending so much time pursuing ballet.

She was invited to participate in a stage performance, along with other students who would be giving various dramatic and musical presentations. She chose a dance to perform for the students and staff of Shenandoah Junior High School. "It was the first time that I had so many of my friends come back and say to me, 'You were really good! You should be going to New York.' It was the first time I was able to show them what I was about and what I was doing. They saw it and they understood it. This event is something I will always remember."

At the age of fourteen, Lourdes Lopez moved to New York with her oldest sister to attend a special school for dancers. Their parents and middle sister remained in Miami. Lourdes was allowed to leave school early each day in order to take three different types of ballet technique classes. About a year later, she met with George Balanchine, a founder and a founding choreographer of the New York City Ballet. As a choreographer, Mr. Balanchine created and designed dance roles. Since Lourdes was not finished with school, she could not become a full company member. At fifteen-and-a-half she joined the New York City Ballet as an apprentice while taking correspondence courses and completing extra work over the next year to finish her schooling. At sixteen, she was accepted into the ballet company as a member of the corps.

According to Lourdes Lopez, one of the highlights of her life was joining the New York City

Ballet. When selecting dancers, certain qualities are desirable, such as being well-proportioned, on the thin side, long legs and arms, well-coordinated, and having a natural sense of movement and rhythm. She recalls, "I grew up with the idea that New York City Ballet dancers had to look a certain way—the blond all-American look. There were also certain physical qualities that were required. I have some of them, but my feet are not perfect ballet feet and certain things about my legs are not a perfect dancer's legs. I thought these things would hold me back from joining the company, but evidently not! It was a big, big surprise and a very happy moment in my life when I finally joined the company. Another high point was being promoted to Principal Dancer."

In 1981, Lourdes Lopez was promoted to Soloist and then just three years later became a Principal Dancer. In a single season, either winter or spring, there are usually seventy-three ballets performed over a twelve-week period. As a Principal Dancer, Lourdes Lopez is responsible for knowing forty to fifty ballets each season. Once a ballet is taught to a dancer, he or she must retain it until it is performed in a few months or years later.

A "casting" paper is posted on the bulletin board with a schedule of the ballets for the coming week. The name of the ballet and the performance dates are listed, as well as the names of the dancers and their roles. Since dancers receive such short notice of their assignments, they must continually

Lopez family photo. Lourdes (far right) is holding daughter, Adriel.

take classes and train in order to be prepared. Almost all principal dance roles require great strength and stamina, along with grace and flexibility. One male principal dancer describes the energy required in a six-minute *pas de deux* (dance for two) as greater than what he needed to go four rounds of boxing in his earlier college days.

Lourdes Lopez works six days a week and may be assigned to as many as eight evening and matinee performances during this time. "As a Principal Dancer I work Tuesday through Sunday. My hours vary—sometimes from ten in the morning until eleven at night. Usually, I have classes beginning at ten in the morning and evening performances. We can rehearse from noon until six—any amount of hours that are necessary, no more than three hours in a row. Sometimes when I don't have a performance, I take my class and come home. Every day of my life can be different in terms of scheduling."

The New York City Ballet company has approximately one hundred members ranging in age from the late teens to the late forties. Although numbers may vary slightly, there are fifty-four dancers in the corps, fourteen soloists, and twenty-four principal dancers. Their two main ballet seasons are winter, November through February, and spring, April through June, with classes and rehearsals in-between. The company's summer home is in Saratoga, New York, where they give performances for about three weeks. Every four or five years the company will travel to Europe for a three-week performance tour. They are mainly based in New York City and will sometimes perform in other cities in the United States, such as Los Angeles and Washington, D.C.

During the 1988 winter season, Lourdes Lopez seriously injured her foot. The surgery in January of 1989 brought a long recuperation period and a chance that she would not be able to return to her

Lourdes with her daughter, Adriel, at Disney World

dancing career. "This was a very traumatic time in my life. With the help of my family, I thought, 'Well this is it. This is what has been given to me. I can go into the surgery and whatever happens, happens. Life has dealt me this and now it is my choice. I can either sit here and feel sorry for myself or change the situation around to see if I can benefit from it.' I thought about the things that I really wanted to do but never could because of dancing."

Lourdes Lopez turned her negative situation into a positive one. Having an interest in child psychology and helping handicapped children through dance, she enrolled in classes at Fordham University. Whenever her schedule permits, she continues to take classes from the University. Additionally, she and her husband, Lionel, an attorney in private practice, chose to start a family. Daughter Adriel was born on November 6, 1989. Two years later, Lourdes was able to work her way back into dancing full-time. Lourdes Lopez credits her husband and daughter for enriching her dancing. She explains that the color and life that her family has added have also become reflected in her style of dance.

Continuing her interest in working with children, Ms. Lopez has become involved with the New York City Ballet Education Department. She has lectured and given demonstrations to fourth-through-sixth graders and high school students in the Tri-State area of New York, New Jersey, and Connecticut. During her visits, she explains to students the differences between modern and classical ballet, how ballet dance roles are created or choreographed to tell a story, and how certain music rhythms fit various ballet steps. She has also written ballet scripts for special Sunday matinee performances which only children are allowed to attend. The ballets are first explained by some of the dancers and then performed on the stage of the New York State Theater. Lourdes Lopez feels that by presenting ballet to children at an early age, their interest, understanding, and enjoyment of ballet are increased.

Looking back on all the ballets Lourdes Lopez has performed, there is not a particular one that she can say is her favorite. Although there are some ballets that she enjoys performing more than others, she points out that when she dances, each performance can be very different. "A performance is not like an ice-cream flavor. If I say, 'I love banana, rocky road,' every time I have banana, rocky road I know what it tastes like. I know exactly what I'm getting. Every single time I perform a ballet I will have a different feeling. Although it is the same ballet, I might hear the music differently this time or I might feel sad that day or happy. All of this affects the performance and it is never the same twice."

Antonia Novello

On December 15, 1992, Dr. Antonia Novello first heard about then President-elect Bill Clinton's plans for her post. Dr. Novello had been U.S. Surgeon General for nearly three years, but Mr. Clinton wanted to make his own appointment to the position. Dr. Novello had wished to continue and was disappointed. While Dr. Novello left her job as Surgeon General at the end of June, 1993, she stayed on as a career officer in the Public Health Service and actually broadened her audience. She became a special representative for UNICEF (United Nations Children's Fund), which would let her help improve health all over the world for women and children.

For almost her entire life, Antonia Coello Novello has concentrated on being a doctor. As a child, she longed to aid those around her. After becoming a physician, she increased her scope through public health. Dr. Novello earned a place in history as the first woman and first Hispanic to become Surgeon General of the United States. Today, she continues her medical mission.

Dr. Novello was born Antonia Coello on August 23, 1944, in Fajardo, Puerto Rico. She grew up in this town, about thirty miles from San Juan, the capital of Puerto Rico. Antonia was eight when her father, Antonio Coello, died. She and her younger brother were brought up by their mother, Ana Delia Flores, a junior high school principal in Fajardo.

"Tonita," as young Antonia was called, knew she wanted to become a doctor and help children, from personal experience. She was born with an abnormally large colon, part of the intestinal system, which did not function properly. This congenital megacolon caused her great discomfort and pain. She had regular medical care, including two weeks of hospitalization each summer, but the defect was not corrected. An operation she was supposed to have when she was eight did not get performed until ten years later.

In the meantime, she endured the condition and admired the doctors who treated her. As a patient, she understood how a few personal words or some extra attention was important. As a potential doctor, she wanted to prevent other patients from having to suffer, as she had, for so long. Her mother encouraged her to lead an active life and to work hard, despite her ailment, and Antonia did not feel limited by her physical problems. Also, her favorite aunt, a nurse, encouraged her to become a doctor.

Antonia attended the University of Puerto Rico in Rio Piedras, majoring in biology and minoring in chemistry. She finally had surgery one summer during college, but complications developed. At one point she left Puerto Rico and spent two months at the Mayo Clinic in Minnesota. Altogether, she had several operations over a period of several years and even lost a semester of studies.

Still, she continued with plans for medical school, and was accepted. Antonia's mother assured her that the challenge of tuition would be met, somehow, and it was. Antonia was on a definite path. She has recalled that her mother did not permit her to have a job until after she had completed medical school, thinking she might be distracted by money and lose focus.

Antonia received her medical degree at the University of Puerto Rico School of Medicine in San Juan in 1970. She was also married in that year, on May 30, to Dr. Joseph Novello. He was a navy flight surgeon who was stationed at Roosevelt Roads Naval Base, close to Fajardo. Together, the Doctors Novello left the warmth of Puerto Rico for the chilly winters of Michigan, as they both went to the University of Michigan in Ann Arbor for more medical training. Her husband specialized in child psychiatry, which deals with mental health.

Antonia representing the Girl Scouts in the annual Fiestas
Patronales *pageant, Fajardo, Puerto Rico, 1957*

Antonia was an intern and then a resident in her chosen field, pediatrics. An additional year at Michigan was spent in nephrology, the study of the kidney and kidney diseases, followed by a year in pediatric nephrology at Georgetown University in Washington, D.C. Antonia had become interested in nephrology after her favorite aunt died at the age of thirty-two of kidney failure. Also, Antonia and some other members of the family had suffered from kidney problems.

In 1976, Antonia started as a clinical instructor in pediatrics at Georgetown University. She rose through the years to become a clinical professor, a post she still holds. Also in 1976, Dr. Novello entered private medical practice in Springfield, Virginia, but this segment of her career lasted only until 1978.

Through her years of training and experience, she had increasingly realized that working for a program could be more effective than trying to help one person at a time. As a pediatric nephrologist, a specialist in children's kidney disease, Dr. Novello had cared for patients awaiting a transplant. She was deeply frustrated at how long it often took to receive a kidney, and that all those who needed help did not receive it, including her favorite aunt. She decided to work in the field of public health, to try to solve these types of problems.

In 1978, Dr. Novello joined the United States Public Health Service, beginning as a Lieutenant in the active reserve. She started work at the National

Institutes of Health (NIH) in Bethesda, Maryland, and was involved with programs concerning artificial kidneys and kidney disease.

In 1982, Antonia Novello received a master's degree in public health, concentrating in health services administration, from Johns Hopkins University in nearby Baltimore. At the same time, she continued at NIH and assisted in reviewing requests for research grants. While assigned as a legislative fellow to a U.S. Senate committee while she was at NIH, she helped with legislation to establish a program to coordinate human organ transplants on a national level, and she helped draft health risk warning labels for cigarettes. Dr. Novello rose in positions at NIH, where she also coordinated research on pediatric AIDS and advised on women's health issues.

Dr. C. Everett Koop had served for nearly two full terms as Surgeon General when he resigned on July 13, 1989. On October 17, 1989, President George Bush chose Dr. Antonia Novello, and on November 1 she was formally nominated to succeed Dr. Koop as Surgeon General of the United States Public Health Service.

Dr. Novello was thrilled. Although the Secretary of Health and Human Services is the highest-ranking health official, the Surgeon General plays a very vocal and prominent role. As Surgeon General, Dr. Novello could advise the entire country on important health issues. She would also lead the approximately 6000-member commissioned corps

of the Public Health Service. The commissioned officers of the health corps are professionals and have ranks similar to the Navy's. They provide a number of important services, such as offering assistance to regions which lack doctors, supporting aid efforts in national emergencies, and conducting research on multiple diseases.

The Surgeon General is chosen by the President and then confirmed by the U.S. Senate. Each term is for four years, with the possibility of reappointment. On March 9, 1990, Antonia Coello Novello

Swearing-in of Dr. Antonia Novello as U.S. Surgeon General, 1990. Left to right: Mrs. Ana D. Flores (mother), Dr. Antonia Novello, Dr. Joseph Novello (husband), President George Bush, Justice Sandra Day O'Connor, Secretary of Health and Human Services Dr. Louis Sullivan.

became the first female and the first Hispanic Surgeon General ever in this country. Wearing her new uniform, with vice-admiral stripes, Dr. Novello was sworn in by U.S. Supreme Court Justice Sandra Day O'Connor at a White House ceremony.

The U.S. Surgeon General gives advice on health issues and seeks to protect public health and safety. In that position, Antonia Novello was frequently in the headlines, citing reports and quoting statistics. Dr. Novello strongly believes that the public should have the necessary information to make the right choices about their health, and they should be aware that their decisions can affect their health for years in the future.

To fulfill her responsibilities, Dr. Novello commissioned research, issued reports, and held news conferences; she publicized research findings and endorsed guidelines recommended by other experts. The Surgeon General also reached audiences by delivering many speeches and writing editorials.

Surgeon General Novello's health concerns covered a wide range, as she warned of health hazards and focused on prevention. She cautioned about the dangers of tobacco smoke, and crusaded against illegal underage drinking and domestic violence. Dr. Novello championed programs to immunize children against diseases and to prevent injuries. She has been concerned with AIDS and drug abuse, especially as it relates to women and children.

Many of Surgeon General Novello's efforts were directed at risks taken by youths. She is very distressed by the number of young people who start to smoke. Most adults who smoke began during childhood or adolescence, and Dr. Novello is afraid that many of today's youngsters will someday die of diseases related to smoking. As Surgeon General, she called for the tobacco industry to stop the kind of advertising which she said appealed to children and teens. Dr. Novello has also warned that smokeless tobacco, such as chewing tobacco, should not be viewed as a substitute for smoking, as it also presents hazards. In December, 1992, she issued a report detailing use of smokeless tobacco by young people, entitled "Spit Tobacco and Youth."

Dr. Novello is also very disturbed about the use of alcohol among youth. Pointing out how packaging and advertising of certain alcoholic beverages can lure teens, she asked for more corporate responsibility from this industry, too. Surgeon General Novello's crusade against illegal underage drinking emphasized links between alcohol consumption and possible devastating consequences. Drunk driving is perhaps the most familiar example, but Dr. Novello warned that alcohol also affects judgment in other areas of behavior, and can be a factor in crime, violence, depression, injury, or taking risks that can lead to AIDS.

Dr. Novello is alarmed at the spread of HIV and AIDS, and quite fearful that many teens do not realize that their behavior today may result in AIDS years later.

Antonia Novello's health concerns stretch in many directions. For example, women's health issues range from the violence against battered women, to lung cancer overtaking breast cancer as the leading cause of cancer death among women, to the practice of excluding women from many health research studies. Her concerns about the health risks of smoking extend to include Latin America, where the habit is on the rise, and she has called for coordinated efforts among countries.

The health needs of Hispanic Americans represent a particular challenge. Hispanic communities in the U.S. represent diversity: people have come from different countries, at different times, for different reasons, and have had different experiences. They cannot all be helped in the same way, whether to prevent AIDS or to address concerns in health insurance. At the request of many Hispanic leaders, an initiative was begun to study the problems and develop solutions.

Surgeon General Novello led the National Hispanic/Latino Health Initiative. First, a national workshop was held in Washington, D.C., in September, 1992. Over 200 Hispanic leaders from various backgrounds discussed issues. Then, a series of regional health meetings involved over 1,000 participants in New York, Miami, Chicago, San Antonio, and Los Angeles. After these meetings, the Initiative Planning Committee met in April, 1993. Results of the workshop and regional meetings were reviewed, and a national plan of action was drafted. On April 23, 1993, Dr. Novello held a news conference and provided the plan's recommendations, which included: increasing access to health care at a community level, collecting better medical information about Hispanic Americans, enlarging the number of Hispanics in science and health professions, and paying special attention to migrant workers' and undocumented aliens' health needs.

Antonia Novello worked as U.S. Surgeon General for over three years. On June 30, 1993, a little over six months after Dr. Novello first heard that

Dr. Antonia Novello, 1990

she would not be asked to stay on, she left her post as Surgeon General. President Clinton's choice for her replacement was Dr. Joycelyn Elders of Arkansas, although the Senate had not yet voted on Dr. Elders' nomination when Dr. Novello stepped down and announced plans for her new position. With UNICEF, Antonia Novello continues her mission of promoting public health while she addresses the needs of women and children, and the topic of health and nutrition.

Dr. Novello and her husband live in Washington, D.C., where he is a child psychiatrist. Her nickname is Toni, and she enjoys collecting antique furniture and attending football games with her husband. She has lamented that her time to exercise is limited, but she takes neighborhood walks and prefers to walk upstairs. Dr. Novello and her husband never had children of their own, but both have helped many children through their careers.

As part of her responsibilities, Dr. Novello has crisscrossed the U.S. and traveled to many countries in the world. Throughout her professional life, she has won numerous awards and honors. In 1994, Antonia Novello was named to the National Women's Hall of Fame in Seneca Falls, New York.

Always, Antonia Coello Novello has been a caring physician, for individuals and on a larger scale. Dr. Novello says that some of her first patients are now her best friends. She will never even meet most of the countless other people whom she has touched and helped.

Ellen Ochoa

WANTED: Men and women who are physically fit, mentally alert, and in good health. Must have college degree in a technical field, a graduate degree or three years' experience in a technical field, and possess strong communication skills. Must be willing to work in small, confined spaces, often in a weightless environment. A good sense of humor is desirable. Those persons who are afraid of heights, hard work, or learning a variety of new technical skills need not apply.

This type of ad would have caught Ellen Ochoa's eye and interest. Instead, graduate school friends told her that NASA was accepting applications to the astronaut training program. Ellen Ochoa wrote to NASA for additional information and requested an application. She had already completed the first requirement, a bachelor of science degree in physics from San Diego State University. She continued to fulfill the technical requirements by earning her master of science degree and a doctorate in electrical engineering from Stanford University. For her doctoral dissertation, Ellen Ochoa developed a special detection system based on optics that was later patented. In January, 1990, she was selected by NASA to enroll in the astronaut training program. In one year, Dr. Ochoa became an astronaut and a future candidate for space shuttle flight crews as a mission specialist. In April, 1993, Ellen Ochoa, who has Mexican ancestry, earned the distinction of becoming the first Hispanic woman astronaut to travel in space, on the shuttle *Discovery.*

Becoming an astronaut was not Ellen Ochoa's childhood dream; her main interests were reading and music. Ellen Ochoa was born on May 10, 1958, in Los Angeles, California. She is the middle child with an older sister, Beth, and older brother, Monte, and two younger brothers, Tyler and Wilson. The five Ochoa children grew up in La Mesa, a suburb of San Diego, California, with their mother, Rosanne Ochoa. Ellen describes her upbringing as "typical middle class," attending Northmont Elementary School, Parkway Junior High School, and Grossmont High School. "I generally enjoyed school. I read a lot. One of the books I remember liking very much is *A Wrinkle in Time.* It was an interesting story about traveling in time. The main character was a girl and she made it easier for me to identify with the story a little bit more. I also enjoyed reading *The Hobbit* series." Outside of elementary school, she took ballet and gymnastics, but only for a few years at a time.

Ellen Ochoa spent most of her free time pur-

Ellen Ochoa at age ten at Mission Bay, San Diego, near her home in La Mesa.

suing her interest in classical music. She learned to play the flute in school and today is an accomplished musician. Music was the common bond among herself and her siblings. "We all played an instrument and one of my brothers, Tyler, sang. We were all in either the marching band, orchestra, or the choir in junior high and high school. Music has been something I've been able to enjoy throughout my life, not just when I was young. When I was in high school I played with the Civic Youth Orchestra in San Diego. In graduate school I gave some solo recitals at Stanford and after that, across the bay in the city of Livermore. More recently I have been playing with a wind ensemble here in Houston, Texas." In 1983, Ellen Ochoa was recognized for her musical excellence as a Student Soloist Award Winner with the Stanford Symphony Orchestra. Later, when interviewing for the astronaut training program, Ellen Ochoa would learn that her accomplishments in music enhanced her qualifications. NASA wants well-rounded astronauts who also have other interests and skills, such as in music, sports, scuba diving, or piloting airplanes.

Even though Ellen Ochoa graduated as the top math student in her high school, no one told her about possible careers where math is put to use. She feels it is essential for students to be given information about different technical careers, especially when a person shows a particular strength or interest. People did not discourage her in high school, but she was not encouraged. "You may not know what you want to do right now or your interests may change or you may learn about a new career later, like becoming an astronaut, that you do not know about today. But it is important to keep your options open and for this reason it is important to study math and science in school. With a good foundation in these areas you will be able to choose many different career paths.

"When I graduated from high school and went

Ellen Ochoa with flute at about age seventeen

to college, I was going to be a music or business major. In fact, I changed my major field of study about five different times—music, business administration, journalism, computer science, then physics. I did not know at that time what I wanted to do." Since she enjoyed math, she started taking math courses in college.

After her first year, Ellen Ochoa talked with a physics professor and an engineering professor to find out which major would be most interesting. A person majoring in physics studies energy and matter and their relationship to mechanics, electricity, magnetics, light, sound, and heat. Engineering concerns the application of basic science to practical purposes. It involves the design, building, operation, and management of technological systems. Engineering spans from traditional fields to medicine and the high technology areas of aerospace, advanced materials, microelectronics, and computers. The traditional engineering fields include electrical, civil, mechanical, industrial, and chemical engineering.

"The engineering professor was very discouraging. He said that a woman had come through his department, once—and engineering is a very difficult subject. I was annoyed that he seemed to think women did not belong in this department. On the other hand, when I talked with the physics professor, he thought I would like being a physics major. He asked about the math courses I had already completed in high school and college and thought

I would be well prepared to study physics. I had not chosen a definite career path and what the professors said and their reactions made an impression on me. The physics department seemed a lot more open and I thought this field would be interesting and challenging. After taking more physics classes, I chose this as my major."

After graduating from San Diego University with a degree in physics, Ellen Ochoa chose to study electrical engineering at Stanford University. By 1985, she had earned a master of science degree and doctorate in electrical engineering. She began working at Sandia National Laboratories and NASA Ames Research Center to gain experience in her field of study before entering the astronaut program. Her work resulted in becoming a coinventor on two different optical processes, each receiving a patent. Dr. Ochoa has been invited to many technical conferences as a speaker and has published articles about her research in different scientific journals.

NASA considers applications for their astronaut program every other year in the odd-numbered years. In order to become accepted into an astronaut training program there are three basic requirements. The first is a college degree in a technical field such as engineering, science, math, or medicine. The second is a graduate degree or three years of experience working in one of the technical fields. The third requirement is to be in good health with no ongoing medical condition which needs medication, and to be reasonably fit. One does not need to be a superathlete to apply.

When candidates are qualified technically and in good health, NASA then looks at other factors. During an interview before a board made up of mostly astronauts, candidates must show that they are confident, pleasant, and able to express themselves clearly, as well as being knowledgable in their technical field. Astronauts spend a great deal of time working with the public, speaking before groups, and visiting schools. They also must be able to live and work with other astronauts in a small area during long-term space travel. The veteran astronauts on the interviewing board look for candidates who are clear thinkers, good communicators, easy to work with, and who have positive attitudes.

Out of thousands of applicants, only the top one hundred are invited to Houston for a week-long health screening and a meeting with the interviewing board. From these hundred, fifteen to twenty-five are finally selected to become part of the NASA astronaut team. The next step is training for space flight.

The initial training program is about one year. During this time everyone takes classes in each shuttle system and attends lectures in related sciences like astronomy, oceanography, and orbital mechanics. Astronauts attend lectures, read, and study. Dr. Ochoa says that it is like being in school. "If you have been a good student, that helps you

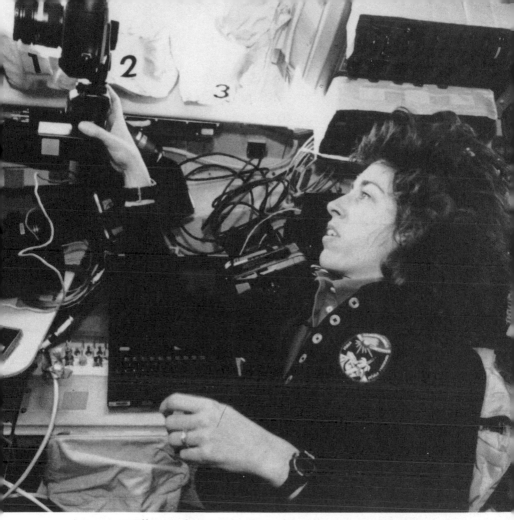

Astronaut Ellen Ochoa is about to take photographs during Discovery's flight in space, 1993.

become a good astronaut. There is so much to learn that strong study habits help you here, just like in school."

Another large part of the preparation program 'ludes learning jobs that support the shuttle program. Each astronaut is assigned a particular responsibility for the shuttle flight; however, this can change from year to year. "The first thing I was assigned to do is to verify the software that is used during flight to control all the shuttle systems. Now, I am assigned to the remote manipulator system which is the robotic arm that we use on the shuttle. But I can be moved to a number of different jobs. That's why NASA looks for people with excellent technical backgrounds where even if you haven't studied some particular aspect of science or technology, you can come up to speed on it quickly enough to be able to do your new job well."

Astronaut trainees also experience simulated shuttle liftoff, flight, and reentry. They even have a chance to experience weightlessness in a special plane, although only for thirty seconds at a time. They also practice making repairs or adjustments to equipment and instruments outside the craft in case of a breakdown or emergency. Wearing pressurized suits, the astronauts complete this training underwater in a large pool or tank, similar to zero-gravity experienced in space. These sessions can last from four to six hours. During each simulated flight or zero-gravity exercise, the astronauts' reactions and response times are recorded and studied.

On April 8, 1993, at 1:29 A.M., Ellen Ochoa, the only woman on a crew of five astronauts, was launched into space aboard the shuttle *Discovery*.

The main goal of this mission was to measure and record the sun's radiation levels and the composition of the atmosphere. The ultraviolet (UV) radiation from the sun causes complex reactions in the atmosphere that can create and destroy ozone. Scientists have been concerned over the reduced levels of ozone in the earth's atmosphere. Ozone, a form of oxygen, acts as a buffer against harmful levels of the sun's UV rays that can cause skin cancer. Humans have created certain chemical products that release ozone pollutants into the air. Chlorofluorocarbons, contained in aerosol sprays, refrigeration units, and in producing plastics can be very destructive.

The scientific instruments that measure the different types and amounts of gases in the earth's atmosphere have been mounted on a large, movable platform. These instruments, known as "ATLAS," have been flown in space before on the same reusable platform. They are to be flown once a year for the next ten years so that changes in the earth's atmosphere resulting from one eleven-year solar cycle can be measured. Part of Dr. Ochoa's job during this mission was to monitor these atmospheric and solar science instruments, make sure they were working correctly, and to issue commands that would help repair or recover the instruments if anything went wrong. The information that Dr. Ochoa helped to record from ATLAS would be added to the data collected over several years and used to find out how the atmosphere changes. In addition, sci-

Astronaut Ochoa taking a musical break from her duties aboard Discovery.

entists will also be able to better determine what causes ozone depletion—how much is due to natural effects from the sun or volcanic eruptions.

Dr. Ochoa's special job assignment aboard *Discovery* was to use the robotic arm to deploy and later retrieve a small, 2,800-pound satellite. This satellite, called Spartan, collected data about the sun's corona and measured the speed of the sun's particles that fall into the Earth's atmosphere. The corona is the bright ring of gases and particles around the sun that can be seen during a solar eclipse. Spartan was launched on the third day of the mission, orbited in space for two days on its own, and then was picked up again by the shuttle.

"Space flight is a great experience!" Ellen Ochoa affirms. "When I was traveling in space, I thought about how lucky I was to be up there and how so many people would want to have the job that I have. Viewing the Earth from space is very special. We had some great views and we took over 8,000 pictures of the Earth while we were orbiting for the nine days. Space flight was about what I expected. When the other astronauts came back, they told us about what it's like, so I felt prepared for the flight by the time I went up. But it is still not the same as being there yourself and feeling what it is like to be in a real weightless environment!"

Each astronaut is allowed two personal items to take with them on their space flights. Dr. Ochoa chose to take her flute, which she was able to play for a short time one day. She also brought a picture of her husband, Dr. Coe Fulmer Miles, who is a research engineer specializing in computer architectures. After completing her first mission in space, Dr. Ochoa had a busy schedule of debriefing with NASA scientists about the data collected, attending special functions to honor her achievements, and speaking before different groups.

Dr. Ellen Ochoa has already received two prestigious awards: the Hispanic Engineer National Achievement Award for 1989's Most Promising Engineer in Government and the 1990 Pride Award given by the National Hispanic Quincentennial Commission. Whenever she has free time she enjoys bicycling, volleyball, and playing her flute. Ellen Ochoa also has her private pilot's license for recreational flying.

Visiting schools is a special part of her job and Dr. Ochoa always brings an important message to students. "When I go around to schools I try to tell students that the way I got this job was through my education. I had no idea when I was younger that this is what I would be doing. Sometimes it is hard to see the connection between what you are doing in school and what you might do when you grow up. In my case, I took an interest in learning and made sure I graduated from high school and college. The type of person NASA looks for is someone who likes to learn new things. There are lots of exciting jobs and careers out there that will be available to you, if you stay in school."

Federico Peña

Marathon runners must have lasting strength, staying power, and the ability to focus on the single task of persisting until the finish. Government leaders must have a strong voice, a mental picture or plan for future growth, and the ability to stick with a problem until solved. Federico Peña, a long-distance runner, became the twelfth Secretary of the United States Department of Transportation on January 21, 1993. Several people have compared his abilities as a runner to the way he tackles and resolves issues that are important to the citizens of our country.

Federico Peña was the third son born to Gustavo and Lucila Peña on March 15, 1947, in Laredo, Texas. The next year brought a set of triplets, two boys and a girl, completing the Peña family of six children. After receiving his bachelor's degree from Texas A&M, Gustavo Peña had begun trading in international markets as a cotton broker. He relocated his family to Brownsville, Texas, when Federico was a young child.

In Brownsville, the Peña children began their schooling. They attended private Catholic school through high school. Federico graduated from St. Joseph's Academy with honors, and was elected to serve in the student government. During high school, Federico was involved in sports. He was a quarterback in football, a second baseman in baseball, and a distance runner in track. With five boys in his own family, enough to have their own backyard basketball team, Federico also excelled in this sport. His younger triplet brother, Alfredo, remembers being very competitive with Federico. The two played baseball and football together in school and enjoyed their friendly rivalry of comparing report cards to see who had the better grades.

Federico Peña entered the University of Texas at Austin in 1964, where he received his undergraduate and law degrees. He was the first in his family to break the chain of graduates from Texas A&M, where his father and two older brothers, Gustavo, Jr., and Oscar, had attended. His triplet brothers, Alfredo and Alberto, joined him later at the University of Texas. He continued his interest in government and politics by campaigning for liberal candidates during state elections and promoting peace during the Vietnam conflict. Earning his law degree in 1971, he began working for a legal aid office in El Paso, Texas.

In 1972, before investigating a job offer in California, Federico Peña visited Alfredo, who was attending law school at the University of Denver in Colorado. Denver triumphed over California and he remained in this city, becoming a staff lawyer for the Mexican American Legal Defense and Educational Fund (MALDEF). Through MALDEF, he connected as legal advisor with the Chicano Education Project (CEP) in 1974. This group's goal was to pass a law that would provide Chicanos throughout Colorado with equal access to educational opportunities. Federico Peña became instrumental in gaining the support of national government for this cause through an unplanned meeting with then Vice President Walter Mondale. By 1977, the first bilingual, bicultural education bill was passed in the state of Colorado and CEP came to an end.

Federico and his younger brother, Alfredo, opened a law office in 1978. Later that year, Federico Peña decided to seek public office. His strong interest in government began in high school and continued through college and into his early professional career as a civil rights attorney with CEP. In addition, his decision to run for the Colorado House of Representatives may have been influenced by his family's ancestors, who had been politically active over one hundred years ago. During the Civil War, his great-grandfather served as Laredo's Mayor. Also, in Laredo, Texas, a great-grandfather was an active member of the first school board and a grandfather was an Alderman, a job similar to that of a city councilperson. After a successful campaign, Federico Peña quickly established a solid reputation as a state legislator. During his two terms in office, he concentrated on issues related to school finance reform, renters' rights, problems between teens and police, and senior citizens. In his second term, he was selected by his peers as the Minority Leader of the Colorado House of Representatives. Having achieved this important and powerful position, Federico Peña was identified by the *Denver Post* newspaper as one of 1981's ten top legislators in the state.

At the end of 1982, Federico Peña was the first to declare his candidacy for Mayor of Denver. When he made his announcement, an informal poll showed that he had a low percentage of voter support. He would be running against two main candidates, the man who had held the Mayor's office for over fourteen years and a former district attorney. Many people said that Federico Peña did not have a chance to unseat the present Mayor, but they were wrong. On election morning, a freak snowstorm blanketed the city. The power was out in many areas and there were many weather-related traffic snarls. In spite of these conditions, the largest voter turnout of the last four mayoral elections was recorded. After the votes were counted there would be a runoff between two can-

Federico Peña, Secretary of Transportation

didates, Federico Peña and the former district attorney.

The campaign grew more intense. Federico Peña received endorsements from the city's largest daily paper, the *Rocky Mountain News,* and from the former Governor of Colorado who also happened to be the Mayor's brother. The Southwest Voter Registration Education Project (SVREP) based in Texas under the leadership of Willie Velasquez, registered about 5,000 new Hispanic voters through a satellite project in Denver. Federico Peña continued to walk neighborhoods and meet people across the city. He gained the support of new residents to Denver, Hispanic residents, young professionals, and several labor groups. His many appearances presented an articulate candidate with refreshing, new ideas that would strengthen Denver's future. His slogan, "Imagine a Great City," caught the public's attention.

On July 1, 1983, Federico Peña, thirty-six years old and of Mexican ancestry, became one of the youngest and the first Hispanic Mayor of the nation's twenty-fourth largest city. Government analysts commented that his success demonstrated the ability of many different groups to unite for a common purpose. He received strong support from Latinos, but they represented less than half the number of votes he needed to win.

As the new Mayor, his first challenge was to deal with the city's over $600 million budget and the approximately $20 million deficit. Recognized for his organization and planning for the short and long term, he developed a timetable that included immediate, three-month, six-month, and four-year goals. His "five-point plan" targeted areas where city costs could possibly be cut, generating savings that would reduce the deficit: review and revise existing city contracts, conduct efficiency studies for each city department, review the city's current investment policies, improve the system for identifying department expenses, and look at possible reductions in upper-level management positions.

At the end of his first term in office, Federico Peña decided to run again. There was a close run-off election which he won by just over 3,500 votes. Several groups were unhappy with what they felt was a lack of progress during the first four years. However, over the next four years the results of the Mayor's careful planning and groundwork became more evident.

In 1988, Federico Peña concluded the drive to build a new international airport in Denver. The old airport, Stapleton, had limited runway space that was considered inadequate in meeting the needs of the city's growing economy and in keeping up with flight schedules throughout the country. Mayor Peña, a Democrat, was able to convince the Secretary of Transportation, a Republican, to help finance the approximately $3 billion project. With its completion, the Denver International Airport would rank as one of the largest in the world and the first major U.S. airport to be constructed in over twenty years. In 1992, Mayor Peña was recognized for his efforts in pursuing this project. The main road from Denver to the new airport was renamed "Peña Boulevard."

Other projects started or completed during Federico Peña's two terms as Mayor include building a new downtown convention center; improvements in public buildings, bridges, and roads; revitalizing a major shopping center; constructing the second-largest performing arts complex in the U.S.; and retaining a bid to bring a major league baseball team to Denver. One of two National League baseball expansion teams was later offered to Denver and named the Colorado Rockies.

Almost all of these enterprises awarded portions of the building contracts to minority firms and provided new jobs during the construction phases, as well as thousands of permanent jobs in the future. Federico Peña has commented that he is especially proud of the Colorado Convention Center being completed on time, on budget, and including a construction firm owned by a Hispanic woman. Environmentalists were also a part of new city planning to ensure progress without harming Colorado's natural beauty. Mayor Peña's further concern for Denver's environment resulted in the use of special fuels and "no drive" days to encourage people to travel to their jobs without using their cars.

Included on the Mayor's list of projects was investigating ways in which Denver could participate

Colorado Governor Dick Lamm and Denver Mayor Federico Peña passing the Olympic Torch in 1984.

in possible trade exchanges with Mexico and Canada. In 1990, Mayor Peña, with a group of Denver business and government leaders, met with the President of Mexico to discuss trade opportunities.

Education has been considered one of Denver's most important investments by Mayor Peña. He has met and encouraged thousands of students, commenting that anyone who pursues an education, hard work and honesty, and has self-respect can make a valuable contribution to society. He has made himself accessible to Denver's youth by visiting schools, scheduling time for students to visit his office, and continuing college internship positions in city government offices.

After serving as Mayor of Denver for eight years, Federico Peña returned to private life, and formed Peña Investment Advisors, Inc. in 1991. Answering the need for minority-owned money management firms, Peña Investment Advisors became one of twenty such companies owned by Hispanics in the U.S. The firm recruited Hispanic professionals in this field to handle an impressive list of clientele such as Pitney Bowes, Southern California Rapid Transit District, and U.S. West, Inc.

Before Federico Peña could fully cultivate Peña Investment Advisors, Inc., he was called to Washington, D.C. He led the two-month, transportation transition team after the presidential election in November, 1992. Having experience in developing city, state, national, and international transportation projects, Federico Peña was readily confirmed by the Senate as the Department of Transportation's new leader. He also fulfilled President-elect Clinton's commitment to nominate cabinet advisors from a variety of ethnic backgrounds and from different parts of the country. He resigned from his position as Chief Executive Officer (CEO) and President of Peña Investment Advisors, sold his shares of the company, and quickly began preparations for his move to Washington, D.C.

Complex airline, maritime (ocean shipping), automobile, and infrastructure (highways, buildings, bridges, railroad tracks) issues faced the new Secretary immediately after his confirmation. In general, Secretary Peña has said that his office will not make more rules and regulations for privately owned companies or move the country to a re-regulated environment. However, he cautions that isolated cases may arise where the government must step in to ensure "fair and reasonable" competition. Secretary Peña intervened in one such case during his first few months in office. A major, well-established airline made plans to compete with a brand-new airline. The larger airline had the ability to charge lower ticket prices that would put the newer airline out of business. The proposed plans were eventually cancelled.

Secretary Peña met with transportation industry and government leaders throughout the United States to identify areas of national concern. The Department of Transportation's budget of over $36 billion a year has been mainly divided among projects to remodel airports, improve air traffic control systems, and upgrade highways and railways across the nation. Recognizing the need to protect the nation's environment, the Secretary meets with experts from the Environmental Protection Agency to discuss the possible impact of these construction projects. The Department of Transportation is also working with U.S. airline and maritime shipping industries to decrease billion dollar losses. Secretary Peña has been in support of the first national committee formed to find possible solutions to the airline industry's problems.

The Transportation Secretary's job leaves little room for scheduling outside activities. Federico Peña spends any free time with his wife and two daughters, Nelia and Cristina. Running and jogging remain an important part of his life. Before the time-consuming Mayor's campaign, he was able to run fifty miles per week. His dedication to running continues with a different look: "I still jog with my entire family, using a 'baby jogger.' " He met Ellen Hart during a ten-mile training race for the 1984 Mayor's Cup in Denver. She crossed the finish line ahead of her future husband and four years later they were married. She had graduated from Harvard University with a fine arts degree and later was graduated from the University of Colorado's School of Law in 1987. Before their first daughter, Nelia, was born in 1990, Ellen Peña founded and directed the Community Action Program, which recruits University of Denver students for volunteer and community service projects.

Like his great-grandfathers before him, Federico Peña has continued his family's dedication to public service. His endurance is tested daily as he leads the Department of Transportation in finding ways to improve transportation systems, modernize city travel facilities, contribute to the nation's economic growth, and compete in a world market—now and in the future.

Matt Rodriguez

The first day at his new job would begin with an announcement of his appointment by the Mayor, but soon thereafter, Chicago Police Superintendent Matt Rodriguez headed to a command center to help save the city from disaster. Torrents of water flooded an underground tunnel system, electricity was shut off, and tens of thousands of workers streamed into the streets. Millions of dollars were lost as property was damaged and business came to a standstill, but order prevailed. There were no serious injuries or deaths. The police assisted in speedily evacuating the problem area and stood guard long thereafter.

The new superintendent's routine tasks were made even more difficult by this instant emergency, but then Matt Rodriguez had spent most of his life leading up to this day. While growing up in Chicago, he had always wanted to be a policeman. At the time of his appointment, he had already been on the force for over thirty years. Twice before, he had been a finalist for the position of Superintendent. Then, on April 13, 1992, he became the first Hispanic American to take command of the second-largest police department in the United States.

Matt L. Rodriguez was born in Chicago, Illinois, on April 5, 1936, the son of Matt L. Rodriguez, Sr., and Annette Rodriguez. His father, of Mexican descent, and his mother, of Polish descent, raised their four children in a South Side neighborhood near the stockyards.

Matt and his two sisters and brother were part of two different ethnic worlds. He says that having these two backgrounds was culturally very enriching. Later in his life, it would be pointed out as an advantage in his dealing with the diversity of the city. As a child, Matt spoke Spanish and Polish. He attended a Polish parochial school and was an altar boy at a Polish church, but he also often served as an altar boy at a Mexican church in the same area.

Matt Rodriguez met Ruth Williams in high school. They were married on April 30, 1955. At the time, he had just turned nineteen and she was seventeen.

Several years after high school, in 1959, Mr. Rodriguez joined the Chicago police force. He started as a patrolman, in uniform, on the North

Side of the city. The following year, he joined the section on Organized Crime as an investigator.

In 1965, Mr. Rodriguez was promoted to sergeant, and for a year he worked as a patrol sergeant. He then took a position as an investigative sergeant in the Criminal Investigations division. In the meantime, Sergeant Rodriguez had been taking classes and working toward college degrees. In 1973, he earned an Associate of Arts degree with high honors in Business Administration at Wright College. During the mid-1970s, he worked as a patrol division watch commander (the officer in charge of a shift, whose duties include reviewing arrest reports, arranging response to emergencies, and scheduling) and later coordinated the gambling unit of the Vice Control division, while he continued with his schooling. He received his bachelor's degree in public adminstration with honors from Roosevelt University in 1975. The following year he completed his master's degree in public administration, also with honors and also from Roosevelt. Sergeant Rodriguez then continued with more postgraduate work at Northwestern University.

Matt Rodriguez was promoted to lieutenant in 1978. While much of his career was devoted to investigating organized crime, gambling, and robberies, he became an expert in the technical side of law enforcement. In 1980, he was appointed Deputy Superintendent of the Bureau of Technical Services. For the next twelve years, he supervised areas which provide technical support to police ac-

Matt L. Rodriguez, Superintendent, Chicago Police Department

tivity. The crime lab, for example, analyzes evidence which has been seized and which police believe to be drugs. Technology aids in transmitting fingerprints of suspects. The 911 emergency system was also under Deputy Superintendent Rodriguez' management.

Also beginning in 1980, Matt Rodriguez went back to the classroom again, but this time on the other side of the desk. As an adjunct professor of criminal justice at the University of Illinois, just south of the downtown "Loop," he taught about organized crime. Soon, he was publishing articles on technical topics, such as the use of mobile computer terminals in the field. In an issue of *FBI Law Enforcement Bulletin*, he described how police departments could evalute and acquire high technology systems, mentioning fingerprint transmission and robotic advances in bomb removal as some examples. For another issue of the same journal, he coauthored an article on a foreign language bank, which is a language resource program combining technology and interpreters. This program lets Chicago police better serve people who speak any of twenty-nine different languages. He also wrote on international drug trafficking, as well as on organized crime. He lectured at conferences both in the U.S. and in foreign countries such as China and England.

Closer to home, he has been chairman of the board of a Chicago area organization called the Hispanic Institute of Law Enforcement (HILE). The group encourages better understanding between local Hispanics and people connected with the criminal justice system, such as the police. HILE holds seminars on topics of interest in the community, such as how to become a U.S. citizen and crime prevention. HILE also actively recruits Hispanic men and women for careers in law enforcement. The Chicago police force was about 3.5 percent Hispanic in 1982, when HILE began. By mid-1993, there were over twice as many Hispanics, about 8 percent, in the department. Chicago itself is about 20 percent Hispanic, and one board member said that a goal of HILE would be to see 20 percent Hispanic representation in the police force.

During the twelve years that Matt Rodriguez was deputy superintendent in the Chicago Police Department, he came very close to the top position twice. In 1983, he was one of three finalists presented to then Mayor Harold Washington by the police board. The other two finalists were Rudolph Nimocks and Fred Rice, and Mr. Rice was chosen by the Mayor. In 1987, when Superintendent Rice announced that he would retire, Matt Rodriguez and Rudolph Nimocks were again two of the finalists selected from fifty-two applications. A special rally was held to endorse Mr. Rodriguez, and his supporters included many area Hispanics of Puerto Rican and Cuban heritages. Some others who offered encouragement were of Chinese and Filipino descent. As Mr. Rodriguez sought the position again, his accomplishments were noted in the press. They included improvements made in the crime lab, motor maintenance, and communications systems. Still, another finalist, LeRoy Martin, was the man picked by Mayor Washington.

In 1992, Superintendent Martin turned sixty-three, the age at which he had to retire. Again, Matt Rodriguez was one of the three finalists. This time, it was Mayor Richard Daley who made the choice from among the three. Citing his expertise and experience, which were necessary to make the force more efficient and effective, Mayor Daley chose Matt Rodriguez to be Superintendent of the Chicago Police Department. His family was invited to attend the official announcement, but Mr. Rodriguez would have little time that day to celebrate.

Officials were alerted to the water leak early in the morning of April 13. Rapidly, basements all over the business district were inundated with over 250 million gallons from the Chicago River. A retaining wall separated the river from a ninety-year-old tunnel system originally built to deliver coal and supplies to downtown buildings, but this wall had ruptured. Water poured through a hole described as about the size of a car. The tunnels still link the buildings forty feet below ground, but now they are used for telephone, cable television, and electrical lines. To avoid electrical short circuits and damage caused when water comes in contact with live electrical systems, electricity was turned off in the entire Loop area.

While Matt Rodriguez' appointment as Superintendent still had to be voted on by the City Council, one of his first jobs as acting superintendent was to deploy officers, some on horseback, to help in the evacuation. Through the night, police pro-

Superintendent Rodriguez (left), Chairman of HILE, and William D. Branon (right), Special Agent in charge of the FBI Field Office in Chicago, presenting the J. Edgar Hoover Scholarship to Lisa Palmer in 1993.

tected property from being looted, as many burglar alarms did not work. Chicago police joined with fire fighters and members of other city departments to keep the disaster from escalating and to safeguard the public. Eventually, the hole was plugged, water was drained out, damage assessed, and life in the business district of the country's third-largest city returned to normal.

With City Council approval in May, 1992, Matt Rodriguez offically became Superintendent. The Chicago Police Department has a force of 12,500, as well as another 3,000 civilian employees. The department has five bureaus, each headed by a deputy superintendent. The largest of these bureaus is Operational Services, which has the Basic Patrol Division. The Bureau of Investigative Services includes the Detective Division and Youth Division. Violent crimes, property crimes, and organized crime are investigated. Vice Control handles liquor, gambling, and other related offenses. The deputy superintendent in charge of the Bureau of Administrative Services is a civilian. This bureau oversees finance, personnel, and data systems. A function of the Bureau of Staff Services is with neighborhood relations. Crime prevention programs are offered, and "Officer Friendly" appeals to children as police officers visit elementary schools to speak about the 911 emergency system, to stress the importance of knowing your own address and phone number, to educate against drug abuse, and lower any fears youngsters may have of the police. The Bureau of Technical Services, which Matt Rodriguez oversaw for twelve years, includes the equipment and supplies of the department, motor pool, communications, and the crime lab.

Geographically, the city is divided into five areas. Each of those is divided into five districts, so there are twenty-five districts to police. Since Chicago has nearly forty miles of beachfront on Lake Michigan, there is also a marine unit, complete with boats. The police department in Chicago is so large that it includes its own polygraph (lie-detector) experts, a unit for bomb removal, and a special team to deal with hostages and terrorists. There is also a mounted unit, with horses, and a canine unit, with dogs.

At times of crisis, as during the flood, Superintendent Rodriguez supervises emergency operations. Other times, he is responsible for many administrative decisions and policies. A recent evaluation of the department recommended having more police work closely with communities. Increasing the number of officers on foot would be of special importance. Superintendent Rodriguez, known for being cautious, did not change policing patterns hastily. Instead, five model districts, which represented the city as a whole, were selected to try community policing. Superintendent Rodriguez also must make budgetary and personnel decisions. Some of his actions during his first year can sound complex, such as reorganizing certain positions and units, and promising new promotional tests to satisfy law changes and get more officers on the job. His post involves planning, forming teams to solve problems, and working well with people.

Then, there are very public aspects of police work. The Chicago flood, response of its police force, and its peaceful outcome were widely re-

Patch with the City of Chicago Seal in the center is worn on the left sleeve by Chicago police.

The Chicago Municipal Flag is on the patch worn on the right sleeve.

ported in the press. Just two months later, the force was in the news again when rioting erupted after the Chicago Bulls basketball team won the championship. Vandals and looters attacked stores and cars, and fires were set. Superintendent Rodriguez had anticipated that trouble might occur and the police were on alert, but over 1,000 people were arrested and over 100 policemen injured. There was some criticism that the police did not respond quickly or strongly enough, but city officials said they had not wanted to provoke problems with very large numbers of police. The following year, the Bulls competed in the finals again. Although the Bulls actually won the title in Phoenix and not on their home court, violence still broke out in Chicago. This time, 5,000 officers in riot gear were already in place, and incidents were not as widespread.

While Superintendent Rodriguez' day can be changed instantly by an emergency, his calendar is full of speeches, travel, meetings, and appearances. He still teaches at the Chicago campus of the University of Illinois. He is also still board chairman of HILF, and in December, 1993, along with William D. Branon, Special Agent in charge of the FBI Field Office in Chicago, presented the J. Edgar Hoover Scholarship to Lisa Palmer. She received this honor while completing her bachelor's degree in criminal justice, with plans to become a Chicago police officer, continue her education and earn a law degree, and then join the FBI. Ms. Palmer is the first Latina from Illinois to win this scholarship. Also in 1993, Superintendent Rodriguez was elected chair of the Major City Chiefs Association, whose member police chiefs come from the fifty highest-populated areas in the United States and Canada's four largest cities. In addition to working with other law enforcement organizations such as the International Association of Chiefs of Police, he has served on state and national advisory committees. In the community, Superintendent Rodriguez is involved with Catholic Charities of the Archdiocese of Chicago, is a board member of the March of Dimes Birth Defects Foundation, and on the board of directors of the Mental Health Association of Greater Chicago. He has been honored with numerous professional and civic awards, including those from the Mexican American Legal Defense and Educational Fund (MALDEF), and Polish, Puerto Rican, and Jewish groups.

In his limited spare time, Matt Rodriguez enjoys watching baseball games and playing golf. He lives in Chicago with his wife, Ruth. They have a daughter, Kathy Rodriguez Diaz, and are grandparents. During that busy day when his appointment was announced, Superintendent Rodriguez still found a moment to let his granddaughter sit in his new office chair.

On a chilly February night in 1993, Superintendent Rodriguez faced a gathering of about 150 people in a Chicago church. He was there to ask the community to assist his police in the area. The people were encouraging, but wanted even more police involvement, as they suffered from a high crime rate. They wanted to be one of the districts selected to test the new community policing program. Superintendent Rodriguez had known this dilemma before, as districts vied to be participants. It was not possible for everyone to be part of the test, but he did feel a responsibility to all residents of the city. He assigned a department member to work closely with these concerned citizens, while the pilot program was being tried elsewhere in Chicago. If the program was successful and established citywide, they would benefit. In the meantime, Matt Rodriguez was there with concern.

Chicago Police Superintendent Matt Rodriguez appreciates advances in technology which allow his department to better fight crime and serve the people. He has expressed care about each individual and knows the importance of police working closely with communities. Whether during a crisis or on a quiet day, Superintendent Rodriguez works to make Chicago safe.

Paul Rodriguez

The radar installation in Iceland was frigid and dark. The site was far north in the world, with a "midnight sun" in summer, but few hours of daylight in winter. Twenty-year-old Paul Rodriguez monitored Soviet submarines as part of his duties in the U.S. Air Force. He was stationed in Iceland, a long way from his Los Angeles area neighborhood. During his four years in the Air Force, his responsibilities included communications operator on a cargo plane, and he rose to the rank of sergeant. He experienced the cultures of Europe as well as Iceland. After his discharge, Paul returned to Los Angeles. In some ways, he was a very different person. He did not want to go back to wasting time on the streets. Instead, he was eager to move forward with his life, go to college, and have a career. However, in at least one way, Paul Rodriguez was the same: always a comic.

In school, Paul had been a class clown. As a teenager, he had used jokes instead of toughness. He would remain a comedian, using his talent over the years to play comedy clubs, for HBO Comic Relief, in film and television roles, and hosting his own talk show. As he became more well-known he expanded to producing and directing, and has used his influence to help in the community. He would like to see more Hispanic themes and performers in the media, and while he entertains, he also works tirelessly for these other goals.

The youngest of five children, Pablo Leobordo Castro Rodriguez was born on January 19, 1955. Mazatlán, his birthplace, is on the west coast of Mexico, in the state of Sinaloa. His father had relatives in the United States, and the Rodriguezes decided to immigrate when Paul was three. Paul's parents were migrant farm workers, and the family traveled from California to Washington State as his parents followed the crops. They harvested fruits and vegetables, including strawberries, lettuce, tomatoes, and celery. Paul remembers both the beauty of country mornings, as well as the harsh cold they experienced when living in shacks without insulation.

When Paul was eight, an accident prevented Paul's father from continuing farm labor. The Rodriguez family settled in Boyle Heights, a section of Los Angeles just southeast of its downtown. That same year, Paul became a U.S. citizen. He recalls that his name was changed from Pablo to Paul by the judge, and says he had no choice.

Several years later, freeway construction forced the Rodriguezes to leave their home in Boyle Heights. They moved from this area to Compton, about ten miles farther south. Paul was already accustomed to making people laugh. However, he says that this move made him even funnier, as he used comedy in a tough neighborhood to break tensions and stay safe. He says he proved himself with jokes, not violence. He could not escape witnessing violence, though, and even saw his best friend shot as he stood nearby.

By eighteen, Paul was very frightened and began to change his life. He had dropped out of high school, but soon took and passed the GED test. He then entered the Air Force, which he says let him encounter more of the world. Overseas, he felt prejudice not as a minority, but as an American, since some foreigners did not like the U.S. He saw poverty and ghettos in other countries, such as Italy, and realized there were hardships and struggles worldwide. In Iceland, with its freezing weather, Paul escaped by reading more. His mother sent old copies of *Reader's Digest*, which he eagerly devoured. He greatly increased his reading skills as well as his curiosity. Also, he met a commanding officer who took a special interest in him. This captain helped him appreciate literature and encouraged him. He suggested that after Paul's discharge

Paul Rodriguez during the program "Storytime" (KCET, Los Angeles) on public television

he should go to a college with ROTC and then re-enter the Air Force as an officer. Sergeant Paul Rodriguez was discharged in 1977, and resumed his civilian life with a purpose.

Paul used the GI Bill, which provides benefits for veterans, and entered community college. He earned an Associate of Arts degree from Long Beach City College and then continued at California State University, Long Beach. He still enjoyed being funny in class, but did not realize that comedy could become his career. One particular teacher recognized his talent and finally persuaded him to try an amateur night at the Comedy Store in Hollywood. He was invited to return, and soon began playing at different clubs. He earned no pay, but hoped to gain experience and be noticed. He was thrilled, but his parents were devastated. They sorely wanted him to finish his education before he did anything else. Paul had been living at home, but they made him leave when he quit the university. Paul says that they did this to try to shock him into recognizing what they thought was a mistake. However, their tactic did not work. Paul continued performing at clubs, fans followed him, a manager soon directed his career, and he toured at colleges.

Paul's humor was aimed at Latinos, as well as the rest of the country. He told many ethnic jokes, and often used stereotypes other people might have of Hispanics. Paul is bilingual, and he presented his act in Spanish or English, depending on the audience. When his manager, who had helped him so much, died suddenly, Paul was very upset. He even stopped performing for a brief period and took a job at a hot dog stand, but then decided to resume. Soon he was telling jokes to television studio audiences. As a warm-up comedian, he was to get the audience in a jovial mood. This led to a small part in an episode of Norman Lear's program, "Gloria," followed by talk show appearances, comedy on cable television, and his first movie role, in *D.C. Cab* in 1983.

Norman Lear had had several successful programs, including "All in the Family" and "Gloria." He wanted to develop a show about a Hispanic family with Paul as its star, and it was called "a.k.a. Pablo." Paul was almost playing himself, a young Mexican-American comedian who quickly rose to success. The similarities between fact and fiction were very strong. His old street and his parents' home were copied for the sets. Paul says that even his bedroom looked the same. Also, Paul's television parents questioned his comedy career and some of his jokes, just like his real parents. Paul maintained that the program concerned a family which happened to be Mexican-American. He hoped it would appeal to a broad audience. He mentioned that another show, "The Waltons," had been watched for its family relationships, not just by people who could relate to its rural setting. "a.k.a. Pablo" premiered in March, 1984, on ABC. Much publicity surrounded the program and its large Hispanic cast. Although the series only ran for six episodes and was not renewed by the network, Paul was thrust into the spotlight more than ever.

Mr. Rodriguez' career broadened during the following years. He steadily had parts in films, including *Quicksilver*, *Born in East L.A.*, and *Made in America*. On television, he had major roles in two other series, both on CBS. For one of these, "Trial and Error," Paul wrote some of the material. He was especially pleased that it was simulcast, as the television provided English while some radio stations broadcast the dialogue in Spanish. Paul also appeared on cable television, including several of his own HBO comedy specials and performances on the annual Comic Relief shows to benefit the homeless. For Fox Broadcasting, he made several specials, including one about prison life and another concerning gangs. He has also been involved in two "Back to School" specials.

To gain more control in the industry, Paul formed a production company with his manager and partner, Jeff Wald. This company has produced a number of Paul's specials, and has ongoing deals to produce other television and film projects. In addition, Paul made his debut as a director in 1993 with a present-day adaptation of "The £1,000,000 Bank-Note," a Mark Twain story set in London. This became *A Million to Juan*, set in current Los Angeles.

Very young audiences have also been able to sample Paul's work. He appeared on "Shelley Duvall's Tall Tales and Legends" on cable. Along with other guest celebrities, he has provided spirited readings of stories, such as *Abuela*, on "Storytime" on public television.

Two very important achievements for Paul Rodriguez have been two very different television programs. One ran for several years and has been shown through Univision, a Spanish-language network, to seventeen countries in Central and South America as well as in the U.S. The other was a play, full of meaning and tradition, in which he performed.

The long-running "El Show de Paul Rodriguez," which premiered in March, 1990, was a talk show with guest entertainers and comedy skits. Mr. Rodriguez served as host and created amusing characters in the sketches. The program was primarily in Spanish, but sometimes was bilingual, as some guests preferred to speak in English. Paul translated any English for his huge Spanish-speaking audience on two continents, and translated Spanish conversation for his English-speaking guests. Also, he says he mixed the two languages when possible. Paul's television presence in Latin America has also boosted his comedy career. He has been invited to perform in many countries as a result of his talent and his language abilities.

The play which has special importance for Mr. Rodriguez is *La Pastorela* ("The Shepherd's Tale"), a Spanish story from medieval times, with good winning over evil. This play was brought across the

Atlantic Ocean by Roman Catholic friars who arrived in the 1500s. While the traditional play was performed many times and in many places over the years, Luis Valdez, Richard Soto, and El Teatro Campesino brought it to the small screen with money from Spanish, British, and American television. Paul was greatly honored to be working on such a project. Paul remembered seeing El Teatro Campesino as a boy, and how his father had stressed the importance of this theater troupe. Since then, it had become even more revered and influential, and offered much involving Mexican-American culture and heritage. Paul's parents were very proud and considered this his most significant work. Paul stars in this piece and was cast with Linda Ronstadt, Cheech Marin, and other noted stars in the filmed, updated version of the tale. Paul played the devil, and appeared in a studded vest adorned by dangling chains. Two menacing horns protruded amidst the curls on his forehead. *La Pastorela* was broadcast in English in the U.S. around Christmastime, 1991, as part of the "Great Performances" series on public television, and then released on video in both English and Spanish-language editions.

Throughout his multimedia career, Mr. Rodriguez has continued to perform stand-up comedy, traveling all over for live appearances. His comedy has evolved to reflect his increased experiences and to suit his wider audiences. His routines now include more than just ethnic humor, as he also dis-

Paul Rodriguez

cusses getting older, travel, dating, and being a single parent. He is doing less of these engagements, however, as he does more producing, directing, and writing. With this direction, he feels he will have more of an influence in the entertainment industry, and he will give his own career much more of a future. Another reason Paul wants to stay closer to his home in Los Angeles is that he can see more of his son, who was born in 1985.

Paul Rodriguez has many professional projects and is also involved in numerous civic and charity causes. He has hosted Spanish-language coverage of the National Leukemia Telethon and has appeared on all six Comic Relief programs. In September, 1992, he participated in a benefit concert in Miami, organized by Gloria and Emilio Estefan to raise money to help victims of Hurricane Andrew. Just days after Los Angeles was jolted by its disastrous earthquake of January 17, 1994, Paul began to help coordinate an earthquake relief show. Funds from this concert would aid the efforts of the American Red Cross. Paul tries to convey the importance of education and the danger of gangs to young people through television specials and also by discussing those topics during other appearances. He is a board member of Education First, contributes to Project Literacy, and is actively involved with the National Hispanic Scholarship Fund.

In turn, the community has recognized Paul Rodriguez. He often hosts or entertains at numerous programs such as the National Council of La Raza's Annual Congressional Recognition Awards, The Desi Entertainment Awards (named after Desi Arnaz), and meetings of the Hispanic Public Affairs Association and National Hispanic Media Con-

While a student there, she became a United States citizen. Ileana completed her Bachelor of Arts degree and later her Master of Science degree, both at Florida International University. She could not speak English when she first arrived in Miami, but she went on to major in English as an undergraduate and received her bachelor's degree with honors in 1975. Following her father, Ileana became an educator. She taught and was also the principal and owner of a private school, Eastern Academy in Hialeah. The school had prekindergarten through sixth grade, with about 130 students. She also became active in professional associations concerned with bilingual education, an interest she would champion. Ms. Ros was still involved with assemblies, schoolbooks, test scores, and recess when she plunged into something totally different.

"I decided to run for elected office because by ___ing a voice for the people I could ensure that ___ir concerns were heard. I wanted to make a pos___ difference in our communities and help people ___ problems they had with the government. Run___ for office is a lot of fun because you meet ___ting people every day." District lines had ___ drawn and many thought the time was right ___ublicans to win seats in heavily Democratic ___unty. Ileana Ros became a candidate for ___ House of Representatives, running in Dis___ ___ West Dade.

___ny other Cuban Americans, including ___ she had chosen the Republican party

ference. Mr. Rodriguez was chosen to receive the 1993 Hispanic Achievement Award in Entertainment.

With all his success, Paul Rodriguez feels that his father is still doubtful about his career. His parents live on a citrus farm in central California, and Paul says that his dad still expects him to get discouraged, leave show business, and help him with the crops. Paul, however, knows differently. He has worked very hard in his acts, in his roles, behind the scenes, and in the community. He likes the direction his life has taken, and intends to continue. He would like even more of a Hispanic presence in the media, even more young people to continue with their education, and to help raise even more money for worthy causes. Paul Rodriguez has made people laugh and has also made a difference.

Ileana Ros-Lehtinen

Seven-year-old Ileana Ros was among the more than a quarter of a million Cubans who fled to the United States between 1959 and 1962. Ileana arrived in Miami, Florida, with her family in 1960. Little distinguished the Ros family from the thousands of other Cuban refugees who escaped the early years of Fidel Castro's regime. Twenty-two years later, Ileana Ros did become unique, as the first Hispanic woman elected to Florida's House of Representatives. When she and fellow Florida State Representative, Dexter Lehtinen, were married, they became the first couple to serve in the state legislature. With more firsts—she is the first Hispanic woman and the first Cuban American to have been elected to the United States Congress—Ileana Ros-Lehtinen has continued to be a symbol and a voice.

Ileana Carmen Ros was born in Havana, Cuba, on July 15, 1952, to Enrique Emilio Ros and Amanda Adato Ros. Her brother was a year old. The same year, 1952, Fulgencio Batista resumed his control of the Cuban government. Ileana's father was a successful educator and her mother was a homemaker, but after Fidel Castro took power in early 1959, their lives changed. Ileana says that a year later they left, in search of freedom that ha been denied. "My family emigrated to the Uni States from Cuba when I was seven years o' was their love of liberty, courage, and sacrif enabled us to face our move to Miami ir distressful a move as possible. The adjus very difficult because we did not know and had no money." They hoped would be temporary, that Cuba come free of Communism, and t' turn. However, this did not ha

Ileana grew up in Miami iles. Her upbringing include Looking back, she says, "' models not only du throughout my life. Th values like respect, h ily values."

Ileana attend with a mix of good studen leader. She vice orgar went first

Ileana Ros-Lehtinen with daughters, Amanda (left) and Patricia (right) in Washington, D.C.

because of its stand against Communism and for freedom in Cuba. She was new to politics, but upset her experienced Democratic opponent in November, 1982. Ileana was the first Hispanic woman in Florida's House of Representatives. She was so excited at learning the results of the election that she said she did not know how she would sleep that night. She was one of several Republican Hispanic-American victors, signaling a shift in Dade County politics. While she kept her position at Eastern Academy, she also made regular trips north to Tallahassee, the capital of Florida.

Dexter Lehtinen, an attorney, was another Florida Representative. He had first been elected in 1980 and represented District 118, near Ileana's. He had been born in Homestead, Florida. They started dating in 1983, after a first outing which included ice cream at a Baskin-Robbins shop. A year later, they became the first married couple in Florida's House of Representatives.

During Ileana's second term in office, their daughter, Amanda Michelle, was born. In 1986, they both decided to seek seats in the Florida Senate. They ran in different districts, saying each would maintain a home in their own district, which caused a bit of controversy. Ileana's father helped with both campaigns, which had the Lehtinens appearing together on television campaign commercials. Once again, they made history. They were the first married couple in Florida's Senate, and Ileana was its first Hispanic member. State Senator Ros-

Lehtinen sponsored a bill helping victims of crime, supported bilingual education, and fought the English Only movement. She also paid special attention to Cuban-American concerns. The Lehtinens presented themselves as a team, sometimes voting similarly on issues and helping each other. Their second daughter, Patricia Marie, was born while they were both state senators. (The girls would sometimes be referred to as A.M. and P.M.)

Ileana longed to run for the U.S. House of Representatives, but Claude Pepper had held his Congressional district seat since 1962 and he was exceptionally popular. She did not wish to challenge him, but wanted to wait until he retired. In 1988, she joked that she hoped he would not retire until her girls were in school. However, a year later, on May 30, 1989, Representative Pepper died at the age of eighty-eight. It was announced that a special election would be held to fill the rest of his term, and Ileana chose to run.

Claude Pepper had been an unbeatable Democrat, but after his death, Republicans felt they could win in his District 18, which covered much of the Miami and Miami Beach area. This district had a large Cuban-American community, which usually voted Republican, including the section of Miami called Little Havana. Ileana Ros-Lehtinen seemed an ideal Republican candidate. She easily won her primary and faced Democrat Gerald Richman. During the campaign, she stressed her record relating to crime and drugs. She emphasized her support of Israel, as the 18th also had a large Jewish population. President George Bush and Vice President Dan Quayle both visited on her behalf, and the President's son Jeb was chairman of her campaign. The race divided along ethnic lines and at times was bitter. As election returns began to come in, results seesawed back and forth. However, when the last ballot was counted, Ileana had won with 53 percent of the vote to Richman's 47 percent.

The victory party that Tuesday night swelled to 1,000 supporters. Famed Salsa singer Celia Cruz stepped up on stage to lead a chant as the crowd waited for their winner to arrive. Just before midnight, Ileana Ros-Lehtinen appeared, along with her husband, parents, and some Republican party leaders. At first she spoke in English, and then switched to Spanish. She said that she wanted those listening in Cuba to hear how our democracy works. Ileana did not get much sleep the night of this victory, either.

Very early the next morning, the Congresswoman-elect was interviewed on the "Today" show. She spent that afternoon with her daughters in the park, but by Thursday morning, she began the task of trying to unify her district. She met with Mr. Richman and other community leaders to repair the divisions of the campaign.

On September 6, 1989, her name went up in lights on the big electronic board used to count Congressional votes. At noon, Ileana Ros-Lehtinen was sworn in as a member of the House of Representatives, as members of her family were among those who watched. She received a plastic voting card and a small, but very special, lapel-type pin to identify her as a member of Congress. She was also given a spouse pin for her husband to wear, to show that he was married to a Congressperson. (For each new Congress, representatives and their spouses receive new, slightly different pins, with the old ones kept as souvenirs.) Ileana began her new job right away. She cast her first vote in the House that afternoon, after meeting President George Bush, who wanted to congratulate her, at the White House.

Her daughters soon left for Miami with her mother, but Ileana hoped they would return to Washington when she found an apartment and a nanny. She also made plans for weekend visits with her husband, who worked in Florida. She looked forward to regular travel to Miami for her constituents and her family.

Representative Ros-Lehtinen had wished for an assignment on the Foreign Affairs Committee, and was thrilled that she received it. She wanted to make an impact on policies concerning Cuba and Israel and the Middle East, topics very important to people of her district. Another of her first choices was the Judiciary Committee, but she was assigned to the Government Operations Committee instead. She was still pleased to work on this committee, and concentrated on employment and hous-

Congresswoman Ileana Ros-Lehtinen at work

ing. She also eagerly joined the Congressional Hispanic Caucus, and became a unique member: its only woman, only Cuban American, and only Republican Hispanic Representative. She welcomed the chance to work with Hispanics from other heritages such as Mexican and Puerto Rican. She hoped that she and these Democratic Hispanics could at least agree on social and educational issues. Representative Ros-Lehtinen had to prove herself fast, because the next election for her seat was just fourteen months away.

This time, Ileana's opponent was Democrat Bernard Anscher. They differed on policies toward Cuba, the Persian Gulf, and the budget. Representative Ros-Lehtinen won her first full term with an even bigger margin, 60 percent to Anscher's 40 percent. She had received seven out of eight Hispanic votes in her district, and also gained more non-Hispanic votes than before. In 1992, her victory was even stronger, with 67 percent of the vote. Her popularity was considered especially strong, since President Bush, at the top of the Republican ticket that year, was defeated by Democrat Bill Clinton. She was reelected again in 1994, this time unopposed.

In addition to taking strong stands on Cuba and the Middle East, Ileana Ros-Lehtinen has also helped with the expansion of the Everglades in Florida and worked to prohibit offshore oil drilling. She is against abortion. She will work for measures, cutting across party lines, when she feels they are worthy. In 1990, she voted for a bill giving family and medical leave, even though President Bush had vetoed it. She strongly favors bilingual voting ballots. In 1992, Hispanic groups joined with Asian-American and Native-American groups to work for passage of the Voting Rights Language Assistance Act. Ileana actively supported the Act and even persuaded some other Republicans to do the same.

In describing her position, Representative Ros-Lehtinen says, "My responsibilities and duties as a Congresswoman entail providing service to my constituents and learning their needs, and working on legislative matters and voting on issues according to their merits." She says that on a typical day, "I read all the mail that is forwarded to me by constituents and my daily work involves reading and acting on this mail, meeting and listening to constituents, and studying legislative proposals and suggestions." Her mornings can include talking with corporate executives and visitors from her district, including high school students touring Washington, D.C., and learning more about government.

As a Congressperson, Ileana Ros-Lehtinen's life is exceedingly busy, with offices in Washington and Miami. "There are always sacrifices to be made when one dedicates oneself to public service Putting the needs and wants of the public and of constituents before mine gives me great pleasure. Having less time to spend with my family is one of

Ileana Ros-Lehtinen, 1993

these sacrifices." However, she tries her hardest to compensate. "My main hobby is spending time with my family. Although I spend some time away from my daughters and husband when I am in Washington, I try to spend as much time as I can with them when I am home and be the best mother that I can be."

When asked to speak to children directly, she says, "I advise young people to always try to do the best they can in their chosen field of study and to follow their convictions and not be discouraged by trials and hardships. I also suggest that they set short and long-range goals for their plans." Her words seem a blueprint for the plan she must have followed herself. The girl who left Havana seized the opportunities and now walks in the U.S. Capitol, proudly wearing her newest Congressional pin.

SELECTED
BIBLIOGRAPHY

The authors interviewed many of the subject people, in person or by phone. In some cases, they corresponded with the subjects in writing, or assistants or family members provided information.

FELIPE ALOU
Blair, Jeff. "Alou Family Sparks Expos." *Baseball America,* October, 1992.
Blair, Jeff. "One Tough Dominican." *The Sporting News,* August 10, 1992.
"The Brothers Three of Baseball." *Ebony,* September, 1965.
Came, Barry. "Up From the Ashes." *Macleans,* September 28, 1992.
Doucet, Jacques. "Felipe Alou: A Real Humane Person in the True Sense of the Word." *Expos Match,* April, 1993.
Marantz, Steve. "The Father and the Son." *The Sporting News,* June 21, 1993.

JAIME ESCALANTE

Chavez, Andres. "Teaching America's Kids: We're All Involved." *Los Angeles Times,* August 26, 1990.

Cohen, Charles E. and Knapp, Dan. "Relocate and Deliver." *People,* September 16, 1991.

Escalante, Jaime A. "A Professional Biography." Written and supplied by Jaime A. Escalante, 1993.

Matthews, Jay. "Escalante Still Stands and Delivers." *Newsweek,* July 20, 1992.

Prado, Mary. "Jaime Escalante: Goodbye to Garfield?" *Hispanic,* April, 1990.

"Success Through Education: Chairman's Award." From the 1989 Hispanic Engineer National Achievement Awards. *Hispanic Engineer,* Conference Issue, 1989.

GLORIA ESTEFAN

Estefan, Gloria. Biographic information supplied by Gloria Estefan, Estefan Enterprises, Inc., 1993.

Stefoff, Rebecca. *Hispanics of Achievement.* New York: Chelsea House Publishers, 1991.

Vachon, Michelle. "Music's Where the Money Is." *Hispanic Business,* July, 1992.

"1993 50 Best Hispanic Restaurants." *Hispanic,* July, 1993.

GIGI FERNANDEZ

Bailey, Sandra. "Winner Doubles Gold." *The New York Times,* August 9, 1992.

Briceno, Carlos. "At the Net with Gigi, Mary Joe & Gabriela." *Hispanic,* July, 1988.

Drozdiak, William. "U.S. Women Double the Gold." *The Washington Post,* August 9, 1992.

Dwyre, Bill. "Team Fernandez Steals Spaniards' Show." *Los Angeles Times,* August 9, 1992.

Woods, Toni Waters. "Higher Education: The Still Rising Gigi Fernandez." *IWT,* August 1992.

ANDY GARCIA

Abella, Alex. "The New Rhythm of Florida." *Los Angeles Times Magazine*, May 23, 1993.

Diamond, Jamie. "Andy Garcia: An Enigma Wrapped Inside Charisma." *The New York Times*, November 22, 1992.

Mansfield, Stephanie. "Andy Garcia Keeps His Shirt On." *Gentlemen's Quarterly*, December, 1990.

Volsky, George. "Andy Garcia Plays Up His Roots." *Hispanic Business*, October, 1992.

ROBERTO GOIZUETA

Heys, Sam. "Goizueta brings own bold flavor to Coke." *The Atlanta Journal/The Atlanta Constitution*, May 26, 1985.

Huey, John. "The World's Best Brand." *Fortune*, May 31, 1993.

Marill, Michele Cohen. "The $59 Million Question." *Atlanta Magazine*, November, 1992.

Oliver, Thomas. *The Real Coke, The Real Story*. New York: Random, 1986; Viking Penguin, 1987.

Ramirez, Anthony. "It's Only Soft Drinks at Coca-Cola." *The New York Times*, May 21, 1990.

Scredon, Scott and Frons, Marc. "Coke's Man on the Spot." *Business Week*, July 29, 1985.

CAROLINA HERRERA

Duka, John. "Notes on Fashion." *The New York Times*, December 30, 1980.

Estrada, Mary Batts. "Carolina Herrera Talks About Fashion." *Hispanic*, March, 1989.

Goodwin, Betty. "Designer Puts Family Ahead of Business." *Los Angeles Times*, January 26, 1990.

Morris, Bernadine. "Openings Without the Fanfare." *The New York Times*, April 13, 1993.

Riehecky, Janet. *Carolina Herrera, International Fashion Designer*. Chicago: Childrens Press, 1991.

Shapiro, Harriet. "From Venezuela to Seventh Avenue, Carolina Herrera's Fashions Cast a Long Shadow." *People*, May 3, 1982.

LOURDES LOPEZ

Flatow, Sheryl. "Ballerina Mother." *Playbill*, November, 1992.

Flatow, Sheryl. "Lourdes Lopez." *New York City Ballet News*, November, 1986.

Hurford, Daphne. "A Pair of Thoroughbreds." *Sports Illustrated*, September 21, 1987.

McFarland, Beverly. "Miami's Lourdes Lopez: Center Stage in New York." *Miami Herald Tropic Magazine*, August 26, 1984.

ANTONIA NOVELLO

Krucoff, Carol. "Antonia Novello: A Dream Come True." *The Saturday Evening Post*, May/June, 1991.

"Novello, Antonia." *Current Biography*, May, 1992.

Novello, Antonia. "My first job was . . ." *Glamour*, September, 1990.

Novello, Antonia C. "Health Priorities for the Nineties, The Quest for Prevention." Delivered at the Town Hall of California, Los Angeles, California, April 21, 1992, in *Vital Speeches of the Day*, August 15, 1992.

Schwartz, John. "Dr. Novello's Steady Pulse." *The Washington Post*, July 2, 1993.

Schwartz, John. "Surgeon General Offers Plan to Address Hispanics' Health." *The Washington Post*, April 24, 1993.

ELLEN OCHOA

Bergheim, Kim. "Coast to Coast: Stars in Her Eyes." *Hispanic*, May, 1990.

Leary, Warren E. "Discovery's Crew Attempts Repairs." *The New York Times*, April 9, 1993.

"Most Promising Engineer in Government." From the 1989 Hispanic Engineer National Achievement Awards. *Hispanic Engineer,* Conference Issue, 1989.
Ochoa, Ellen. "Biographical Data." Supplied by NASA, 1993.

FEDERICO PEÑA

Arias, Anna Maria. "Federico Peña: Quick Study." *Hispanic,* June, 1993.
Bradsher, Keith. "Clinton's Last Selections for the Cabinet Reflect His Quest for Diversity." *The New York Times,* December 25, 1992.
Flynn, Kevin. "Peña's political rise cheered in Texas." *Rocky Mountain News,* June 14, 1983.
Greenhouse, Steven. "Confirmation Roundup." *The New York Times,* January 8, 1993.
Martinez, Chip. "Federico Peña: Denver's First Hispanic Mayor." *Nuestro,* August, 1983.
Ronquillo, David. "Man With a Plan." *Hispanic Business,* April, 1993.

MATT RODRIGUEZ

Kamin, Blair. "Rodriguez boosted for top police post." *Chicago Tribune,* September 15, 1987.
McRoberts, Flynn and Martin, Andrew. "Looting, violence mar night to celebrate." *Chicago Tribune,* June 21, 1993.
Rodriguez, Matt L. "The Acquisition of High Technology Systems by Law Enforcement." *FBI Law Enforcement Bulletin,* December, 1988.
Rose, David James. "Chicago's Top Cop." *Hispanic,* May, 1993.
Stein, Sharman. "Sink or swim." *Chicago Tribune,* June 21, 1992.
Wilkerson, Isabel. "Chicago's Loop Is Closed Down As Riv-

er's Water Floods Tunnels." *The New York Times*, April 14, 1992.

PAUL RODRIGUEZ

Knutzen, Eirik. " 'Pablo Is Much Like Me.' " *Nuestro*, April, 1984.

McLellan, Dennis. "Road Weary." *Los Angeles Times*, January 14, 1993.

Moran, Julio. "Taking Comics Seriously." *Los Angeles Times*, in "Nuestro Tiempo," a bilingual section, February 11, 1993.

Padilla, Steve. "The Comedian." *Nuestro*, March, 1983.

Rohter, Larry. "To Bethlehem by Way of Mexico, With Linda Ronstadt in Wings." *The New York Times*, July 28, 1991.

ILEANA ROS-LEHTINEN

CQ's Political Staff. Duncan, Phil, Editor. *Congressional Quarterly's Politics in America 1992, The 102nd Congress.* Washington, D. C.: CQ Press, 1991.

Cartagena, Maria José. "Ileana Ros-Lehtinen." *Intercambios Femeniles*, Summer, 1988.

Gonzales, Enrique J. "Breaking the Beltway Barrier." *Hispanic Business*, April, 1993

Soto, Luis Feldstein. "A pair of aces." *The Miami Herald*, September 6, 1989.

Soto, Luis Feldstein. "It's Ros-Lehtinen, 53–47%." *The Miami Herald*, August 30, 1989.

Zaldivar, R. A. "Ros-Lehtinen joins House amid cheers." *The Miami Herald*, September 7, 1989.

INDEX